What Does The Lord Require?

Meditations On Major Moral And Social Issues

James L. Killen, Jr.

CSS Publishing Company, Inc., Lima, Ohio

WHAT DOES THE LORD REQUIRE?

Library of Congress Cataloging-in-Publication Data

Killen, James L.
What does the Lord require? : meditations on major moral and social issues / James L. Killen, Jr.
p. cm.
ISBN 0-7880-2306-3 (pbk. : alk. paper)
1. Sermons, American. 2. Christian life—Meditations. I. Title
BV4241.K475 2004
252'.076—dc22

2003022218

For more information about CSS Publishing Company resources, visit our website at www.csspub.com or e-mail us at custserv@csspub.com or call (800) 241-4056.

ISBN 0-7880-2306-3 PRINTED IN U.S.A.

To all people everywhere
who hope for a better world
and
to Mada,
my partner in all that I do

Table Of Contents

Preface

What has happened to us? While we were looking away, our world has started falling apart. Just when the cold war was over and the power and prosperity of our country was rising to new heights, just when we thought our churches had nothing better to do than to promote their own growth and to compete at trying to market the most entertaining worship services, just when we thought everything was okay, a succession of catastrophes has overtaken us. Terrorists crashed hijacked airliners into The World Trade Center, the Pentagon, and a field in Pennsylvania, killing thousands of innocent people and forcing us to recognize that there are millions of people in this world who hate us. Soon after that, the American people found their nation engaged in an armed conflict that seems to have set us at odds with most of the rest of the world. Then several major corporations collapsed because of the corruption of their top executives, leaving many unemployed or impoverished and destroying the nation's confidence in the structures of business and government that we all need to be able to trust. There is a growing awareness that many of the systems that deliver essential services, like medical care, legal service and insurance, are in trouble because of the abuses some people have made of them. With these tragedies as a wake-up call, we have looked around and discovered that everything really isn't okay. There are lots of things that are wrong in our world and in our lives. There are lots of big issues that have not been getting the attention that they should have been getting.

Most of us have not yet fully taken in all of the meaning of the things that are going on around us. But as the realization emerges, we will become increasingly aware that the world needs to hear again some of the nearly forgotten implications of the Christian message. The world needs to hear again the good news that God is at work in our lives and in our world to save us and all people from everything that prevents or destroys life in its fullness. The world needs to hear again the call of God to live up to the very highest possibility that God has opened to us. And the world, especially the people of conscience in the world, even more especially those who are committed to Jesus Christ, needs to hear the calling of God to participate in the saving work that God is doing in the world.

People of good conscience will need to ask again, "What does the Lord require of us?" The prophet Micah answered, "To do justice, love kindness and walk humbly with your God" (Micah 6:8). Jesus answered, "... you shall love the Lord your God with all your heart, and with all your soul, and with all your mind, and with all your strength," and "You shall love your neighbor as yourself" (Mark 12:29-31). But just what will it mean for us to live up to these requirements in all of the unique specific situations of our lives and in all of the emerging situations of our world's history? Christians must be constantly trying to think and pray their ways through answers for that question, "What does the Lord require?"

The meditations in this collection were originally prepared and delivered as sermons intended to help Christian people find their way to an understanding of the requirements of God with regard to the great social and moral issues of our day. Most were prepared for the congregations of Williams Memorial United Methodist Church in Texarkana, Texas, and Trinity United Methodist Church in Beaumont, Texas. You will be able to guess what kinds of occasions originally evoked these sermons. They have been revised in an attempt to make them as relevant as they can be to the ever-changing realities of life in today's world. Four of the sermons were previously published in other forms in *Preaching Magazine* or *Pulpit Digest.*

I would like to express my gratitude to all of the congregations that evoked these sermons and sometimes participated in producing them, to Stan Purdum and Teresa Rhoads and all of the people at CSS Publishing Company who gave me the opportunity to have this book published, to Bishop Joe Wilson and General Hiram Jones who critiqued my manuscript, and to my wife Mada who corrected my spelling.

These meditations are offered to you to help you answer for yourself the question about what the Lord requires of you. In the Appendix, there are questions that may be used to stimulate group discussion. Of course, we cannot claim to have spoken "the last word" on any of these issues. The situations in life that require our response are forever emerging and changing. And the answers that are required cannot ever be adequately formulated in terms of words and concepts. The answers required must take the shape of commitments of the heart, and of decisive action, and of lives lived in faithfulness to the purpose of God. Indeed, they must take the shape of responses to the specific requirements that God addresses to us through the emerging situations of our lives and of the history of our world. People of good conscience will always be asking and listening with their whole being to learn just what the Lord requires of us.

Once To Every Man And Nation

Esther 4:13-17

Once a churchman wrote a letter to his pastor. He sent him copies of several articles he had clipped from news magazines mentioning the involvement of their denomination in several social issues. In his letter, the man asked, "Why is our church involved in things like that?" Lots of people wonder about that. But, in fact, things like that are part of what the Christian faith is about. Yes, it is about personal salvation, but it is also about God working to change the world and make it better.

Throughout the Old Testament and the New, the Bible describes God as being at work in human history to move the creation toward the fulfillment of its highest possibility. In this, God does not work either by miraculous intervention, at least not usually, or by inevitable "progress." Instead, God works in subtle ways through the movements of human life and history. God works through the aspirations and struggles and suffering of people. God works through the crises that emerge and are resolved in ways that determine the future course of human history. And God calls us, the human creatures that are involved in the drama of life and history, to participate with God in the shaping of the future. That is an important part of what the Christian faith is all about. It is a demanding and difficult and sometimes dangerous thing in which to be involved, but it is a part of the higher humanity to which God calls us.

It seems that this call to involvement is especially binding upon American Christians. In a democracy, people get to decide what their country will do. American people can make a difference. If they don't, it is because they have chosen not to. Furthermore, American people take pride in being committed to high principles like liberty and justice for all.

There is a great hymn, based on a poem by James Russell Lowell,[1] that speaks eloquently of this aspect of our faith:

Once to every man and nation comes the moment to decide,
In the strife of truth with falsehood, for the good or evil side;
Some great cause, God's new Messiah, offering each the bloom or blight,
And the choice goes by forever twixt that darkness and that light.

Times for decision come to us all. Do you know the story of Esther from which our scripture reading was drawn? Esther was a beautiful young Jewish woman who lived with her uncle, Mordecai, in the capital city of the Persian empire during the days when Persia ruled most of the ancient world. One day, during a great festival, the wife of the king of Persia did something headstrong that embarrassed her husband, so he put her away from him and sent people to seek the most beautiful young woman in the empire to take her place. Esther was chosen. The king evidently did not know that she was Jewish, nor did he care. He took her to be his wife. Esther, the Jewish girl, moved into the palace to live in the midst of luxury and power.

About that time, a wicked man named Haman, who was in the court of the king, devised a plot to get the king to order the annihilation of all of the Jews in the empire. Mordecai got wind of the plot and he sent word of it to Esther and asked her to intercede. Esther sent word back that it would not be so easy. If any person went to the king without having been called by him, that person would be killed unless the king graciously extended his golden scepter to him or her. It would be very risky to go to the king uninvited.

Mordecai urged Esther not to feel secure in her position but rather to think of it as an opportunity to do something decisive for the good of her people. He said, "Perhaps you have come to this royal dignity for just such a time as this." Esther responded bravely. She asked that all of the Jewish people fast and pray for three days. After that, she would go to the king and take the consequences. She said, "If I perish, I perish."

Esther did risk her life and go to the king. He received her graciously. She was able to foil the plot and to save her people. To this day, Jewish people remember her courage when they celebrate "Purim."

Every time matters of justice and human well-being are at issue, God calls God's people to act courageously. God gives us every position of advantage that we may have to enable us to serve truth and justice more effectively. But there is always the temptation to love our positions of advantage so dearly that we are unwilling to risk them. The song goes on:

> *Then to side with truth is noble, when we share her wretched crust,*
> *Ere her cause bring fame and profit and 'tis prosperous to be just.*
> *Then it is the brave man chooses, while the coward stands aside,*
> *Till the multitude make virtue of the faith they had denied.*

For many years, the American people were tempted, as was Esther, to retreat into the safety and advantage that our country's geography and power have given us, and to separate ourselves from the suffering and turmoil that oppress much of the world. It was easy for us to forget about what others were suffering and to believe that our own virtue had bought us our good fortune. But then the tragedy of September 11, 2001, occurred. We will all remember forever the image of the towers of The World Trade Center crumbling. We were forced to realize that we are not safe. We are part of the world in which things like famine and poverty and oppression and slavery and "ethnic cleansing" happen. John Donne told us the truth when he said:

> *No man is an island, entire in itself; every man is a part of the continent, a part of the main; if a clod is washed away by the sea, Europe is the less, as well as if a promontory were, as well as if a manor of your friend's or of your own were; any man's death diminishes me because*

I am involved in all mankind. And therefore never send to know for whom the bell tolls; it tolls for thee.

There are three ways in which we may react to that discovery. We can deny it and try to reassemble our illusions of safety and virtue or we can follow our natural inclination to let anger rule us. We can give in to thinking that sending in the bombers can solve the problem or we can recover the challenge of our faith, to ask what God is trying to do to make things better in our world and to look for ways of becoming participants in that work.

It is no small or easy thing to choose that third alternative. Down through the years, people who have chosen it have found it costly and dangerous. Are we willing? Our country is governed by the decisions of the people. God calls us to act courageously in the service of truth and justice for all. There have been times when we have done it. But we have to wonder if we are still willing. Does it worry you that "Once to Every Man and Nation" has been left out of many of our latest hymnals? Was it really because some of the wording was offensive to the women's movement or was there another reason? Are we getting addicted to our comfort and our advantage? Are we becoming too self-indulgent to follow the way that the hymn calls us to go?

By the light of burning martyrs, Christ thy bleeding feet we track,
Toiling up new Calvaries ever with the cross that turns not back.
New occasions teach new duties, time makes ancient good uncouth;
They must upward still and onward who would keep abreast of truth.

That doesn't exactly sound like the theme song of our culture, does it? We are a people who are becoming more and more self-indulgent and committed to our own advantages. But there are still matters of truth and justice and human well-being that are in the process of being decided. Are we willing to answer the call of God to participate in the decision making?

If we are, we will have to start by asking hard questions. What about our culture? It really isn't healthy, is it? Lots of people seem anxious to list the symptoms of its sickness. They talk indignantly about moral laxity and loss of morale, the break up of families, teen pregnancies, drug abuse and drug traffic, corruption and crime. You know the oft-repeated catalogue. But no one seems willing to call into question the materialistic and self-seeking way of life that is the root cause of so many of our problems. We are not willing to let that go and we are not glad to hear anyone call it into question. It would take great courage to make a difference in that.

And are we willing to take greater responsibility for the policies of our own nation? Once a group of American Christians had to listen to one of their members, who was a new American, explaining that she had not always loved America. She had grown up in Nicaragua. She told about her childhood experiences during the war there. She told about looking out the window and seeing the bodies of her neighbors killed without reason by the soldiers, and about the soldiers coming to her house and her mother begging for the lives of her children, and about the great number of men who were either killed in the war or who just disappeared. Then her American friends heard her say she was told that our country had supported that. That was awfully hard for them to hear. But it is necessary to know about things like that and to understand them and to make decisions about them.

It is terribly hard to say anything critical about our country, especially when it is being attacked by both enemies and critics. We want to rally to the support of our country and to shout in its defense. And, in fact, many of our neighbors will think it is unpatriotic for us to do anything else. But if things are to get better in the world, we need to be willing to look inward honestly.

And yet, repentance alone will not solve all of the world's problems because they are not all within us. After we have reckoned with all of the wrongness in our lives and in our communities and in our churches and in our country, we will have to recover our confidence in God and in ourselves and in our God-given purpose. We will have to venture out courageously to find ways of acting decisively in the service of God's loving purpose for the whole creation.

The crises that call for decisions that will shape the future of the world come swirling toward us in unpredictable succession, like whirlpools in a rapid river. Will we be able to rise to the occasion? Will we see our advantages as an opportunity to do something to make a difference for good — or will we draw back from decisiveness in order to protect our advantages? The future of the world, and the character of our nation — and our own character — will depend upon our willingness to participate with God in moving our world toward the fulfillment of its highest possibilities. It can be dangerous. It can be costly. But there is a promise in it:

Though the cause of evil prosper, yet 'tis truth alone is strong;
Though her portion be the scaffold, and upon the throne be wrong,
Yet that scaffold sways the future, and behind the dim unknown,
Standeth God within the shadow, keeping watch above his own.

---

1. James Russell Lowell, "Once to Every Man and Nation," *The Book of Hymns* (Nashville: The United Methodist Publishing House, 1964), No. 242.

God's "No"

Exodus 20:1-17

We modern Christians like to think of ourselves as people who practice a positive religion, one that puts the emphasis on the "Thou shalts" rather than on the "Thou shalt nots," especially the one that says, "Thou shalt love." We think that a life that is shaped primarily by a bunch of "no-nos" would be stifling and joyless. We think that life ought rather to be shaped by hearing and believing the great "Yes" that God speaks in love to us and to every person. That *is* a good way to think about the Christian faith. But yet — but yet — there is still a great "No" that is part of God's interaction with us, and we need to hear it and to heed it because to ignore it is to put ourselves and the whole creation in serious jeopardy.

That great "No" is God's response to everything that is contrary to God's loving purpose for us. God wants for us, and for the whole creation, life at its very best. We were created to live up to the very highest possible level of humanity and to maintain God's creation in beauty and justice and goodness. God's "Yes" rests upon everything that builds up and moves the creation toward the fulfillment of that purpose. But God's "No" must rest upon everything that is hurtful or destructive to us or to the rest of God's creation.

This "No" that we are talking about is not just some moralistic little prohibition. It is a great convulsion, choked with divine anguish. It is like something that originates in the most distant part of the universe. It rushes toward us giving the galaxies a spin as it comes. When it strikes, it makes the mountains quake. And, if our humanity is not dead, it reverberates in our own minds and echoes back as a "No" that is our own. It is the horrified reaction of one who loves to all that destroys what is loved. And even when it is translated into laws written on stone by the very hand of God, it loses something in translation.

What kind of thing could evoke that kind of response from God? The most conspicuous example we can think of is war. Many of you have been to war and you know what it is like. The rest of us can only imagine what it is like on the basis of what we have heard. Our imagining tells us that it must be horrible. It turns beautiful countrysides into desolation and cities into rubble. It destroys the infrastructures that both God and humans have created to sustain life. It regards God's most beautiful and precious creations, human beings, as disposable. It piles their lifeless bodies up like cordwood, having undone the miracle of the creation of life. It attacks the humanity of all who are involved in it. It doesn't matter whether it is a primitive conflict fought with handheld machetes or a sophisticated modern warfare in which deadly missiles are aimed at populated areas by people sitting at computer consoles so far away that they can't see the destruction they cause. The effect is the same.

Some parts of the Bible say some very bewildering things about God being involved in warfare. But if God really is the loving God whom we know through Jesus Christ, there cannot be any war that does not break the heart of God.

Now please understand that nothing we are saying is intended as an attack on those brave people whose names are carved on that black marble wall in Washington — or on the thousands of red granite monuments on courthouse lawns all across this country. They are victims of the tragedy as surely as are little girls burned by napalm. Soldiers are somebody's children, too. They are victims, too. Those who are required to die are victims of one kind and those who are required to kill are victims of another kind — and some of you sitting here know what that means.

Can anything be more horrible than war? Can't we all see clearly that God's "No" rests upon it? And yet, we have so clothed our wars with the noble trappings of patriotism that we often fail to hear the "No." We do that to make it possible for us to endure what tragic history sometimes makes necessary. But we do that at great risk. When we silence the "No" we may begin to think of war as an acceptable way of accomplishing national objectives. Some, who wage crusades and jihads, even go to war in the name of religion. In the Middle East, in Northern Ireland, in Bosnia, and in other places, we have even seen people go to war to oppress and destroy and rape and kill in the name of the Christian religion. How can anyone who knows anything about Jesus do that? When God sees that, God's response must certainly be a great, heartbroken, "No, no, no." And we put the whole creation in jeopardy when we refuse to hear it.

One certain pastor led his congregation in praying their way through the war in the Persian Gulf. A number of members of his congregation had family members or loved ones serving in or near the action. As a church family, they prayed their way through that terrible time. Generally, they made the assumption that their country's involvement there was a tragic necessity, something made necessary by criminal aggression. But when the war was over, the pastor was chagrined to see that the victory celebration suggested that some were making political capital out of the tragedy. He felt that he had to say something from the pulpit about celebrating the end of a tragedy in the same way one might celebrate a high school football championship. He knew that some would not like it. And some didn't. But after the worship service, two men, who were older than the pastor, came around separately and privately and said, "Preacher, I am glad you said that. These people don't seem to realize that we killed thousands of people over there." Both of those men had flown bombers during the Second World War. One had been a pilot and one had been a bombardier. They were brave men who did what they felt they had to do in the midst of a tragic time in the world's history. But they still dared to let themselves hear God's "No" resting upon the whole war — and they didn't pretend that it was right or good — and they didn't let themselves forget how bad it was.

Where does this divine "No" come from? It comes from the same place as the divine "Yes." It is the other side of the divine "Yes." It is not just a legalistic prohibition. It is like the awful "No" that rises in the heart of a parent who drives past a traffic accident and realizes that the small car that has just been crushed by an eighteen-wheeler is the one they bought for their children to drive.

Fortunately, very few parents actually have to experience that — but every parent imagines it. And, kids, in case you are wondering, that kind of imagining is the origin of most of those troublesome restrictions your parents impose on you while you are growing up. It may help to know that your parents make up all of those "thou shalt nots" because they love you and they want to keep you alive and on the right track toward a healthy and happy life.

In just the same way, those divine "Thou shalt nots" arise out of God's "Yes" to all that is good for us. Commandments like "Thou shalt not kill," "Thou shalt not steal," "Thou shalt not commit adultery," and the rest come from the aching heart of God who loves us and knows what can happen to us. The things they prohibit are things that could wreck our lives.

But this was not supposed to be a sermon on war. That is just one conspicuous example of the kind of thing that evokes a great "No" from God. What are some other examples?

Famine must be as repulsive to God as war. This world is able to produce enough food to feed its whole population. Yet, time and time again, political oppression, or greed, or short-sightedness plunge whole parts of the world into famines that cause little children to grow up mentally retarded because of malnutrition and that threatens adults with the slow, agonizing death of starvation. Till yet, when we see their emaciated faces looking at us from the covers of news magazines, we hear God's "No" echoing back from deep within ourselves and we send aid. But there is danger that we could slip into "compassion fatigue" and that our selfishness could make us stop hearing the "No."

Let's face another of the knotty problems of our day. How does all of this apply to abortion? That issue is really much more complex than the most vocal protagonists on either side of the argument want to admit. It is foolish to say that an unborn child is just tissue that can be disposed of if it is troublesome. It is a person. Just ask any mother who is going through a wanted pregnancy. To that mother, the fetus is a person and the mother loves it and wants for it to be born into a loving family and to grow up into a healthy, happy, productive person. We can believe that God feels that way about every unborn child. Yes, there are some tragic human situations that may make the termination of a pregnancy the lesser of two evils. But nothing can make it really right. And whenever a person, either born or unborn, dies short of human fulfillment, no matter what the reason, that is the occasion for great grief in the heart of God. Anyone who is having to make a decision about an abortion needs to take that into consideration. Not to do so is to lose part of our humanity.

God's "No" rests on many different human situations. It probably rests upon some things that we don't think about, things that our culture has taught us to think of as acceptable. It rests on things like young people having everything they need to make life wholesome and good but trashing it all in the pursuit of some attractive pleasure. God's "No" rests on things like families having all of the advantages that should enable them to build strong, loving family relationships but letting that slip away as one of the casualties of their pursuit of material prosperity. When we see that sort of thing happening, we should hear God sobbing. We will all be wise to stay sensitive to the sadness of God.

Well then, what are we to make of all of that? It really doesn't translate into any simple rules for living. It is still true that life shaped by "Thou shalt nots" alone will be a stale and joyless existence. It is true that the big question must always be, "What does love require?" And it isn't enough just to say, "Always do what is right and never do what is wrong." Life won't let us live that way. Life is always dancing us into situations in which we are forced to decide which is the lesser of two evils. And it is not always easy to know what love requires. Time and again, decisiveness will require us to choose between options that are all at least partially wrong.

But in those times, we ought not to tell ourselves that what we are doing is right or good. We ought always to let ourselves hear God's "No" when it comes through. We will be wise always to let it be part of the conversation that shapes our decisions. And when we find God's "No" resting upon our actions, we can let it send us looking for God's forgiving grace — and for God's saving work — and for God's guidance to show us a better way. At the very least, continuing to hear God's "No" can keep our humanity alive even in the most compromised of life situations. It is important to know that, because God's "No," like God's "Yes," is a gift of love.[1]

---

1. This sermon was originally published in *Pulpit Digest*, March-April, 1998, David Albert Farmer, Editor (Inver Grove Heights, Minnesota: Logos Productions Inc.).

How Can I Love My Country?

Exodus 31:18; 32:1, 7-12, 30-34

How can Christians love their country? How can an American Christian love America?

That must sound to many people like a very curious kind of question. It may seem like a curious question, indeed, to at least two groups of people for different reasons.

Some people have so merged religion and patriotism that they will want to respond, "How can a Christian *not* love his or her country?" To them, the Christian faith is a part of the American way of life. Their motto is, "America, love it or leave it." Of course American Christians must love their country!

Another group of people are so obsessed with the shortcomings of America that they may respond, "How, indeed, can a Christian love a country like this?" They see this country standing under the righteous judgment of God for all sorts of reasons. They think that to love such a wicked country would be to compromise their love for God.

Most of us feel that there is something wrong with both of those attitudes. We know there are lots of things wrong with our country. Yet, we feel that there must be some way of loving our country that does not set us at odds with God.

There is a story in the Old Testament about a man who learned from God and from a lifetime of experience how to love a nation. His name was Moses. Moses can show us all how to love our country.

Moses was an Israelite. But, when God first began to deal with Moses, complicated circumstances had separated him from his people. God found Moses living and working as a prosperous shepherd in the land of Midian, far from the place where his people were being forced to do grueling labor as slaves of the Egyptians. One day, as Moses was alone, keeping the sheep in a deserted place, God called out to him. God got his attention by appearing in a bush that seemed to be burning. God spoke to Moses through the bush and said, "Moses, I love your people — and your people are suffering. I care about that. And, I want you to care about it, too. I want to send you to help your people." After some argument, Moses obeyed God. He left the safety of Midian and owned his oneness with his own people.

Those who love God are called to love those whom God loves. Love that is real is not just an abstraction or an emotion. It is a commitment that accepts responsibility and responds to needs. And, real love cannot be lost in generalizations. If you really love all humankind, you have to express it by responding lovingly to those who are near you, those who are most dependent on you, like your family — or your neighbor — or your country. This country of ours is part of that world that God so loved that "he gave his only son ..." (John 3:16). Loving our country is part of our assignment from God.

But God did not call Moses to love his country in comfortable detachment. God sent Moses to get decisively involved in the life of his people in a stressful and costly and dangerous way. God sent Moses to march up to the most powerful king on the face of the earth in that day and say, "Let my people go." God sent Moses to win the confidence of a disorganized and disillusioned people and to persuade them to follow him out into a dangerous wilderness in an unimaginable adventure. God sent Moses to lead the people through forty years of hardship toward the fulfillment of some purpose God had in mind for them. None of that was easy.

God expects more than just passive patriotism from American Christians, too. This nation is not already what it is to become. It is, by history and by constitution, a nation in the process of becoming. It will be what its people make it. God sends us to be decisively involved, each in his or her own way, to give leadership to this nation, to make a difference in it, to help it become what God wants it to be. That won't be easy for us either.

Moses had not gone far as the leader of his newly-liberated people before he realized that they were a hardheaded, unappreciative, and rebellious bunch. At the very time when they should have been most attentive to their relationship with God, they rebelled. They were camping beside a great mountain near the place where God had first called Moses. Moses had gone up on the mountain to represent the people before God. And, God had come to meet him to make a covenant by which Israel would be the chosen people of God. That was a great time. You would have thought the people would have been waiting in breathless reverence. But, instead, they got tired of waiting. They made themselves a little homemade god and indulged themselves in an orgy that they called worship. It became the duty of Moses to express his love by taking his people to task for their wrongness and by disciplining them.

Lots of people think that to love your country means never to see or to say anything bad about it — and certainly never to criticize national policy. But our country is not perfect. Anyone who is at all in tune with God will know that there are lots of things wrong with this country: a self-seeking, materialistic value system, a disregard for basic morality, arrogance in the use of power, a lack of commitment to economic justice for all people, and many other things. Things like that can weaken a nation and cause it to fall. The best favor people who really love their country can do for their country is to cry out against its wrongs and try to get their country to change. God calls us to love our country like that. But that cannot give us an excuse to act superior or self-righteous.

Moses demonstrated an even greater love for his nation when the people of Israel behaved in a way that brought the wrath of God upon them. When God saw that the people had broken the covenant even while it was still being made, God was on the verge of rejecting them. He said to Moses, "This has been a mistake. These people will never be the people I have called them to be. I am going to cut them off and start over with you, Moses. I will make my chosen nation out of your descendants." Moses could have disowned his people and gotten an advancement. He could have gone from being just the leader to being the patriarch, the father of his country. But, he wouldn't do it. Moses continued to own his oneness with his people, even when that meant putting himself under the wrath of God with them and suffering with them the results of sinfulness in which he had not participated. Moses stood with Israel and interceded with God for Israel. He asked God to forgive Israel. And, he said, "Lord, if you can't forgive them, just blot me out along with them."

American Christians need to learn that kind of love for their country. We are to try to lead the country into righteousness. Sometimes we have to try to be righteous on behalf of the country. Then, when, in spite of all of that, the country brings suffering upon itself because of its unrighteousness, we must be ready to suffer with it. How easy it is for us to say, "Don't blame me. It wasn't my fault." The real lover of a country stands with the country in its suffering and prays for the country that it may be forgiven and saved.

In just such heroic love, Moses spent his whole life, representing God to his people and representing his people to God. He spent his life leading the people and following God. Through forty years of wandering in the wilderness, he led them toward the fulfillment of a God-given destiny that neither he nor the people could yet even visualize. Then, when Moses had finally spent himself, when his human shortcomings and his mortality finally caught up with him, Moses loved his nation enough to let it go on without him. Standing on a mountaintop in the land of Moab, Moses saw the Promised Land in the distance, and there he died.

To love our country in that way is no treachery against God. We are called to express our love for God through that kind of love for all humankind. And love that is not just an abstraction always has to start with that segment of humankind that is most ready to hand. Are we up to loving our country in the way in which God calls us to love it?

There was a very meaningful contemporary model of that kind of love for country in a movie that came out in the aftermath of the war in Vietnam.

In the last scene of the movie *The Deer Hunter*, a small group of young men and women gathered in a bar where they had so often shared youthful celebrations of life. But this time, they have gathered in grief, to share a meal after the funeral of a friend. It is clear that they are mourning much more than the loss of their friend.

Only a few months before, three young men had left that town to fight for their country in Vietnam. They went surrounded with the love of their families and friends. They went with the cheers of the local V.F.W. Post ringing in their ears. They went with the same mixture of youthful love for adventure and patriotic devotion that has moved young men to go to war in every generation.

Then they experienced the horrors of war in Vietnam. They saw human life turned into something cheap and very tentative. They experienced the bitterness of their country's first defeat, evacuation from the embassy roof. They endured the jeers of anti-war protesters who called into question the rightness of the whole involvement.

One of the young men returned with both legs blown away by a land mine. One returned physically well but with deep emotional scars inside of him. The third returned dead. He had not died in battle. He died because he shot himself in a game of Russian roulette while he was in a drug-induced stupor.

The two remaining soldiers and their friends gathered for the funeral of the one who had died. They were all suffering, in the depths of their being, all of the devastation and disillusionment of what must have been one of our country's darkest hours. They had loved their country deeply and decisively. They had suffered for their country. They had suffered with their country. They had even suffered at their country's hands. But as the film ended, they joined in singing, "God bless America, land that I love. Stand beside her and guide her through the night with a light from above."

We don't like our patriotism like that. We like our patriotism with flags flying and bands playing triumphant marches. But there are a lot of young people who, like the characters in the film, learned a greater kind of love for country, the same kind that Moses had learned so long ago.

Can Christians love their country? Yes. It is not only permitted; it is required. But it is not easy. Let us pray that God will make us able to do what God calls us to do.

Christian Citizenship In A Pluralistic Society

Psalm 33; Luke 13:20-21

"Happy [blessed] is the nation whose God is the Lord" (Psalm 33:12). The Bible, especially the Old Testament, has a lot to say about the importance of keeping strong the religious heritage of a nation. Many of us who are American Christians believe that message is as important for us as it was for ancient Israel. We are a blessed nation. If our nation is to continue to be blessed, we must somehow see that we continue to be "one nation, under God." In a pluralistic nation, where not everyone shares the same religious heritage, it is not easy to know how to do that. But there is a way. It is not an easy way, but it is an effective way. And the future of our country may depend upon our following it.

People of every nation can appropriately apply to their own countries the biblical teachings having to do with the chosen people of God. It is especially easy for Americans to see their country in the light. Like ancient Israel, our country is made up of people who came out of various forms of oppression in the Old World. Our country had its experience with the wilderness, where life is formed more by the essentials of humanity's experience with reality than by social and political traditions. And those who laid the foundations of our nation drew heavily upon the biblical traditions that asserted the human dignity of every person. Even now, even though the affirmation has been called into question, most Americans continue to know ourselves as "one nation, under God, indivisible, with liberty and justice for all."

Since we know ourselves in that way, it is easy for us to hear the biblical prophets speaking to us when they warn, time and again, that the nation that remains faithful to the Lord will remain strong and free and the nation that forsakes the Lord will fall.

But it is not as easy to do that in twenty-first-century America as it was in ancient Israel. Lots of different kinds of people live here and they do not all share the same religious heritage.

There are some people who have a very clear understanding of how they think we should keep our religious heritage strong. Some of them are probably friends of yours. They think we should reconstruct a religion that comes as close as possible to the Calvinism that was dominant during America's colonial days and then write its requirements into our laws, teach its precepts in our schools, and require everyone to conform to it. They want to say to everyone, "This is the religion that made our country great. Either accept it or go somewhere else."

That sounds like a good idea to lots of people, but there are several things that are wrong with it. In the first place, it is based on a faulty memory of what things were like in colonial days. There was a lot more pluralism around back then than our friends seem to remember. And that pluralism made its valuable contributions to our national heritage.

But the most important problem is that there are lots of different kinds of people in our country today. Most of us who are Methodists think it would be great if everyone in the world were a Methodist. Baptists and Presbyterians and Episcopalians probably have similar opinions. But that is not the way things are. And all of those Muslims and Hindus and Jews and Catholics are not going to go back where they came from. Some of them have been here for a long time. They think this is their country, too. Besides that, there are lots of people who do not profess any religious faith at all and they think this is their country.

And we really think that, too, don't we? Isn't that a part of what we think America is supposed to be, lots of different people living together in mutual respect? Even if that is not a part of what we believe about America, we are stuck with a religion that teaches us to love our neighbors and to do to others what we would want others to do to us. We would want others to respect our religious convictions, even if we were a minority group, so we have to be ready to respect the convictions of others.

It won't be possible for us to give religious undergirding to our country by just writing the teachings of our religion into our national traditions and requiring everyone to conform to them. It does seem that we can recognize secularism as a religion and ask our government not to make any laws that establish that as the religion of the land. We can ask our country to make space for the practice of our religion. But we can't ask to have our religion established as the religion of the state either. That really is not the best way to do it anyway. The experiences of ancient Israel and of the American colonies will teach us that, if we will listen carefully to them.

There is a better way. If the citizens of a country who are Christians will enter into vital, life-shaping relationships with God and live their faith in all of their relationships, their influence will be greater than any formalities they could get written into law. If we will really live our faith, we will function like the leaven in the parable that Jesus taught. We will be a change agent that mixes into the society of the nation and makes it different, just as a little bit of leaven, or yeast, mixed into a large lump of bread dough, changes the nature of the whole thing (Luke 13:21).

If all of the Christians of the country would work harder at living the faith we profess, our influence could have an impact upon some of the most urgent needs of our nation.

If we live as people of faith, we can renew the confidence of the nation. There is a lot of bewilderment and anxiety around these days. People look at the world in which we live and at the future that is coming toward us and they are afraid. Do you remember the great anxiety that gripped the nation as it anticipated the coming of the year 2000? There has been even more anxiety since the tragedy of September 11, 2001. It is fear that makes people want to narrow the structures of life and to make everyone else conform. It is fear that makes us unwilling to be open to that which is different and unknown. It is strange that we should experience that kind of fear at a time when our country is undisputedly the strongest country in the world. But power brings its own dangers with it. There is a lot of that kind of anxiety at work in our country.

The Christian faith puts us in touch with a great and loving God who has the present and the future in divine hands. It was trusting that God that enabled the people of Israel to move out of the safety of slavery in Egypt and to travel into the wilderness expecting to be led to a better future. Venturing out in faith, trusting the living God, is an important part of what the Christian faith is all about. If there are enough American citizens who have learned to face the future in liberating trust, we may be able to renew the confidence of the nation. It is much better to find courage through trusting the living God than to find safety through trusting the formalities of our religion.

If we live as people of integrity, we may be able to heal the cynicism of our nation. It is no secret that many Americans have been so frequently disappointed in leaders and in the institutions of government and business and community and religious life in our world that they are reticent to trust anyone or anything. The collapse of the Enron Corporation and the implication of their accounting firm did great damage to the ability of Americans to trust. The ones we should have been able to trust have let us down too often. There is widespread cynicism among us. This is especially true among young people. That cynicism has seduced many into thinking there is nothing to do but look out for yourself, and so they have thrown away their own integrity. When that happens, people find safety in regarding everyone who talks about higher values as a hypocrite. And yet, we are all hungry to find something we can believe in. We yearn to find some integrity that will let us believe in humanity — and in ourselves again.

Citizens who live their Christian faith will live as people of integrity. We who know about the forgiving love of God will be able to be honest about our own shortcomings. We who know about the promise of God will want to live up to the highest humanity we know about. We who remember the God-given purpose of our government and business and social and religious institutions will be more anxious to achieve those purposes than simply to achieve institutional success. Christians and churches will have to go some to learn to live as examples of real integrity. We have sometimes let the people who trusted us down, too. But it is one of the important things we can do for our nation. We can give all of the disillusioned and compromised people of our world something they can believe in — and a reason to begin again to believe in themselves.

And if Christians learn to live as people of conviction, we may be able to renew the conscience of our nation. It is no secret that the structures of ethics and of morality are breaking down in our society. The dominant culture seems to say, "Forget about what is right or wrong. Just do whatever is expedient or profitable or pleasurable for you or for your party." In this culture, fewer and fewer people seem to care about the ethical and moral teachings of the church. They are likely to resent any mention of them. A couple of years ago, when the state of Texas embraced the dubious practice of depending upon the gambling industry to solve its revenue problems, a high government official commented that religious convictions did not seem to be a significant factor in the decision making.

We have already said that we can't just write the teachings of our religion into law and require everyone else to conform to them. But if we actually live like people who march to the beat of a different drummer, and if we let our Christian convictions influence the way we vote, we can recover some moral influence. If, instead of shouting about conforming to religious laws, we argue that people should have a loving regard for justice and for the dignity and well-being of all people, we may recover some of the lost moral and ethical influence that the church once had.

This will not be easy. It will require us to be different. People who find it expedient or profitable to do things that we may find objectionable will call us hypocrites. But the truth is that most people know that our country needs to recover its conscience. They realize that things are falling apart because of our loss of our sense of right and wrong. If we go about it with humility, and respect for others, our world may be glad to see Christian citizens trying to revive the conscience of the country.

If we were able to live out our faith in these influential ways, the Church, and the faith it professes could win back some of the ability to influence society that we have lost in recent years. Do you remember the story of Mother Teresa of Calcutta? She demonstrated the way in which a Christian who lives the faith can influence a whole country.

India is probably the most pluralistic country on the face of the earth. It is predominantly Hindu but there are large populations of Muslims, Sikhs, Parsees, and other religions. Bitter experience with violent religious conflicts have caused the country to impose some strict limitations on the ways in which a religion can influence the nation. In that country, Christians are a small minority group and they have the disadvantage of being identified with the colonial power that once ruled the country.

But one little nun of Eastern European origin got the attention of the country and of the world by leaving the security of her convent and moving into the slums of Calcutta to care for the poor people who were left to die on the streets of that city. She saw in each needy person a representative of the Christ and of God's call to loving service. She and the followers who gathered around her lived out such an example of sacrificial love that India came to believe in her. A Nobel prize called the attention of the world to her work. Her influence and her ability to do good increased as people responded to her example. She was real. She had integrity. She was living in love. And India felt itself being humanized by her presence. They listened to what she had to say. Her Christian faith made a difference in a land that made no pretense of being a Christian country.

There is a Christian song from the '60s that may indeed teach us how to become influential again in our nation and to make a difference. The song says: "... they will know we are Christians by our love."

"Blessed is the nation whose God is the Lord." The best way for Christians to win that blessedness for their country is to live out the life of love in our citizenship and in every other relationship.

Economic Justice, Facing The Issue

Amos 2:6-8, 5:11-15; Matthew 6:31-33

For years, they had all been hearing that our world's economic system is working in a way that makes the rich richer and the poor poorer and that it is reducing the disadvantaged people of the world, especially of the "developing nations," to deep, oppressive poverty. They had all heard the prophetic messages of the Latin American "theologians of liberation" saying that God is partial to the poor and that Christian people ought to join with the poor to work to eliminate the causes of their poverty. But, for many of the 3,000 delegates who came to Rio de Janeiro, Brazil, for the 1996 World Methodist Conference, these things had not yet become real.[1] In Rio, they could look around and see what the prophets had been talking about. They saw the squatter's villages, they call them "favellas," filling every empty space and climbing up the steep mountainsides in view of the fine homes of the affluent and of the luxury hotels where the lunch buffet costs 25 American dollars. Thousands of people live as well as they can in these favellas. Two hundred thousand people live in one favella alone, the favella called "Prosthemia." These people are in poverty, not because of any failure of their own, but as a result of economic conditions beyond their control. The conference was especially concerned about the thousands of children who come, or are sent, down from those squatters' villages to live on the streets of Rio to get money by working, by begging, and sometimes by stealing. These street children represent a major problem that impacts every country in the world. Furthermore, more and more people are realizing that the problem of economic inequity is not just "someone else's problem." There is reason to believe that the conditions that caused the widespread poverty in Latin America are spreading to other countries — including our own.

Today, we are going to talk about the knotty issue of economic justice. We are going to ask questions about what kind of a response Christian people ought to make to the suffering of the poor people of the earth.

Right now, many of you are probably thinking, "Why do we have to think about that? Economics is a complex subject. Economic justice is a disturbing issue that asks uncomfortable questions about our way of life and that do not allow for any simple or clear cut solutions. Why do we have to think about that, especially in church? Why can't we stick to the spiritual things?"

The answer is that we have to think about economic justice because God wants us to. The Bible makes that clear. People who read the Bible through for the first time are often surprised at what they find there. A certain affluent American professional man participated in a nine-month comprehensive Bible study that caused him to read and study most of the Bible for the first time. He had an unexpected experience. He was surprised at how much the Bible says about money and about economic justice. He was deeply disturbed by the fact that he heard the Bible contradicting some of the things our culture had taught him. He had grown accustomed to being encouraged to "get all you can for yourself and leave others to look out for themselves." He had always believed that was the American way of life and that the Christian faith supports the American way. But he heard the Bible saying, "God wants everyone to have enough, and God wants us to want that, too." In genuine anguish, the man asked his pastor, "Does the Bible condemn capitalism?"

Actually, the Bible does not condemn capitalism as such. It seems that most of the Bible is set in social systems that functioned according to a sort of primitive agrarian capitalism. Some people think that they see the development of a kind of socialism in the early church in Jerusalem. The book of Acts tells us that "all who believed were together and had all things in common; they would sell their possessions and goods and distribute the proceeds to all, as any had need" (Acts 2:44-45). But, if you read that passage carefully and in context, it will be apparent that it is an example of Christian stewardship and of sharing rather than of socialism. The biblical people practiced capitalism. Yet they knew that, left to itself, economics will work to the advantage of the rich. It can move toward a kind of feudalism in which a few rich and powerful people have all of the resources and the rest of the population is reduced to servitude and desperation. They had seen that happen in Egypt and in the cities of Canaan. They knew that God wants something better than that for God's people.

This commitment to the well-being of all people is apparent in many parts of the Bible. The Old Testament books of the law (Torah), which shaped the life of the Jewish nation, required farmers to leave some of their crops to be gleaned by the poor, the widows and orphans, and the disadvantaged. They were reminded again and again that their ancestors had been poor sojourners in Egypt (Deuteronomy 24:19-22). Limits were set on what the rich could do to exploit the poor. Later, the prophets thundered God's condemnation upon those who violated these commandments. Amos cried out against those who would sell the needy for a pair of shoes and trample the heads of the poor into the dust of the earth and push the afflicted out of the way (Amos 2:6-7). Isaiah condemned those who increase their holdings, adding house to house and field to field until there is no room left for anyone else (Isaiah 5:8). Jesus called his followers to be responsive to the needs of the poor saying, "I was hungry and you gave me food ... Truly I tell you, just as you did it to one of the least of these, who are members of my family, you did it to me" (Matthew 25:31-45).

You just can't read the Bible without knowing that God wants all people to have enough and that there is something wrong with any situation that reduces some people to desperate poverty.

When we look around at our world with that in mind, it becomes apparent that there is something wrong.

The delegates to the World Methodist Conference could travel around in the city that was once thought to be a very glamorous place and see not only the poverty of the poor but the impact of that poverty upon the quality of life in the whole city. They knew that they were meeting in Rio because economic and political conditions in neighboring Argentina were so volatile that it seemed unsafe for the meeting to be held in Buenos Aires. In fact, the economic conditions we have been describing were the reasons for the revolutionary movements that had broken out in places like Bolivia, Nicaragua, and El Salvador.

In Mexico, our near neighbor, nearly half of all of the children who die before the age of five die of malnutrition — while one of our biggest problems continues to be overeating. There is a lot of suffering in our world.

And here is something that really spells the problem out. Several years ago, the basketball star, Michael Jordan, was awarded a contract for twenty million dollars a year to endorse Nike tennis shoes. That is more than the entire payroll of the factory in Indonesia that makes Nike tennis shoes. There is something wrong with that, isn't there?

To our embarrassment, even though the vast majority of American people would never intentionally exploit or oppress anyone, the systems that tend to impoverish the disadvantaged people of the world work to our advantage.

But now another dimension of this problem is developing. The same tendency for the rich to get richer and for everyone else to get poorer is present in our own country.

Early in the preparations for the 1997 presidential campaign, candidates for the nominations of both parties finally said out loud what many of us had been knowing for a long time. Most average Americans are less prosperous today than they were twenty years ago. We are moving down the ladder of affluence, not up. And for many people, this is devastating. (Somehow that issue got lost as the campaigns developed. It has not emerged again since. Politicians don't like to talk about this.)

In part, this is a result of the globalization of the economy. When the average daily wage of workers in Asia and Latin America is three dollars and the average daily wage of workers in the United States is 85 dollars, the shrinking of the world is bound to have a negative effect on American prosperity. We have all heard the frequent news reports of the closing of American manufacturing industries and the relocation of those operations to other countries where labor costs are lower. In a competitive business situation, that may seem the expedient thing to do. But its impact on the families of the American workers who were displaced can be destructive.

There are evidently some other forces at work to make the rich richer and the rest poorer. The companies call it "getting lean and mean" to stay competitive. It involves reducing staff as much as possible and requiring those who are retained to work more for what they get. It also involves replacing highly paid employees with employees who can be paid much less. You have seen it happening. Recently, a man standing in line at the grocery store told a friend about the second job he had taken to make ends meet. He ended by saying, "Even at that, I don't make as much as I made before I was laid off from the plant." Where is this leading?

On November 6, 1995, Lester Thurow published an article in the *New York Times Magazine* that gave a statistical analysis of what is happening to us. He said that, in the past 25 years, the difference between the incomes of the top twenty percent of the wage earning men and the bottom twenty percent has doubled. In a time when gross domestic production rose by 29 percent, the real earning of working men fell by eleven percent. The share of the wealth held by the top one percent of our population is double what it was in the mid-1970s. One percent of the country's population now owns close to forty percent of the country's resources. Thurow ends by asking the question, "Can democracy survive that much inequity?"[2]

The trend has evidently continued. On May 17, 2002, Bill Moyers hosted a television documentary that dealt with the widening gap between the rich and the poor in America. He said that so much money is being sucked up into the pockets of the richest one percent of the American population that America has now become the most unequal of the industrialized nations. The very rich get richer, but the workers are impoverished. His program had several sections. In the first, there was a report on the growing income gap in Hartford, Connecticut, where, since 1990, the average income of the top fifth of the population has increased by 21 percent and that of the lowest fifth has declined by nineteen percent. In the second segment of the program, he interviewed Kevin Phillips, author of *Money and Democracy*, who asserted that big money has been able virtually to buy control of both of the major political parties in our government. Then there was a brief segment on the lavish lifestyle of the very wealthy followed by a report on the spiraling cost of medical care. We have come to a place where forty million Americans can no longer afford health insurance. Moyers ended his program by saying that "the rich have declared class war and spent what it took to win ... All that is left now is for the politicians to divide up the spoils."[3]

When we put all of these things together and think about where they may be leading us, we catch a vision that is so frightening that most of us don't want to look at it. But we must look at it. And, we must ask where it is going.

In 1996, Jose Miguez Boninos, who is a theologian and a pastor in Argentina, said that economic conditions in his own country have gotten so bad that those who once thought of themselves as the affluent are finding their own fortunes impacted. Doctors and lawyers are finding their waiting rooms empty because people cannot afford their services. He said they are responding differently. Some are becoming bitter and dropping into despair. Others are finally seeing things more clearly and joining the poor in a search for solutions. Since that time, conditions have gotten worse. (At the time of this writing, Argentina is bankrupt and in a state of dangerous political turmoil.)

Unfortunately, some respond in violent ways. We have experienced the results of the fanaticism that was born out of desperation in Afghanistan. And some don't know any way to respond to a threat but through repression. Some people who arrived early for the World Methodist Conference in Rio employed a guide to take them to see some of the work that the churches were doing with the street children. The guide took them first to a place near a Catholic cathedral where someone, possibly the police, had recently found seven young girls sleeping on the sidewalk and shot them as they slept. The places where they lay were outlined in yellow paint and above them on the cathedral wall was written the word, "unrequited," because as yet no one has been punished. That story should fill us all with anguish. We wonder, "Is that where the history of the world is going, toward a time when we just get all we can for ourselves, oblivious to the effect of our getting on others, and when the children of the poor will be regarded as rubbish to be disposed of?"

Then what should Christian people do about these conditions? Let us hasten to say that there are no simple solutions. The problems are too complex. But there are three things that we can do that will be steps in the right direction.

The first thing we are most naturally inclined to do is one right thing to do. Americans, and especially Christians, just naturally want to respond to human need in compassion. While some treat the poor like rubbish to be disposed of, the Christian churches in Brazil see them as precious children of God and are committing massive efforts toward rescuing them and helping them break the cycle of poverty. Thousands of street children are fed and involved in school programs every day through the efforts of the churches in Brazil. The first letter of John asks, "How does God's love abide in anyone who has the world's goods and sees a brother or sister in need and yet refuses to help?" (1 John 3:17). Giving help is one right thing to do. But there are others.

One that we may not have thought of is that we need to prepare ourselves to be spiritual survivors in this world of changing economic conditions. You see, many of us have gotten addicted to upward mobility. It would not be so bad if we had just made a game of seeing how much we can accumulate. The problem is that we have made a religion of it. It is where we find the meaning of our lives. It is where we get our sense of basic well-being. Consequently, an end to easy upward mobility can be really devastating. It has been for many people.

We need to discover a new way of putting our lives together, a new center around which to organize them. Jesus gave us the key when he said, "... do not worry about your life, what you will eat or what you will drink ... But strive first for the kingdom of God and his righteousness and all of these things will be given to you as well" (Matthew 6:25-33). These familiar words were never more relevant than they are now. If we take them seriously, they will enable us to live full, good lives under any economic conditions. We will be able to survive downward mobility as whole persons and to show others how to do that, too. We may actually be set free to make sacrifices if we have to in the quest for economic justice.

Then we must participate as best we can in the search for solutions to the economic problems of our world. The way to economic justice has not yet been found. And we can suppose that, when it is found, it will not be something easy or simplistic. Bishop Peter Storey of the Methodist Church in South Africa made a profound brief statement. He said, "We can assume these issues are complex, but the principles of Jesus are not." If those who work among the complexities of economic life will work with a loving commitment to the well-being of all people, the solutions will eventually emerge. If the leaders of business and government — and the rest of us, too — learn to ask, "How can we see that the needs of all people are met?" instead of just asking, "How can we maximize our own profit and that of those we represent?" the solutions will eventually emerge. It will take a conversion of culture to lead the decision makers to think in those terms. But God may be working through conditions in the world to lead us to be open to that kind of conversion. Let us pray that it comes in time.

From the private dining room on the fourteenth story of the Intercontinental Hotel in Rio, one can catch a very meaningful vision. A broad street runs between the high-rise apartment buildings where the affluent live. Their tennis courts and swimming pools and manicured lawns are surrounded by walls with guarded gates to keep intruders out. Then the street crosses a freeway and gets lost among the makeshift dwellings of the favella where several thousand people live in oppressive poverty. The houses climb the steep banks of a mountain. But beyond that mountain, in the distance, one can see the top of another mountain and on top of that the massive statue of Christ the Redeemer with arms outstretched that dominates the city of Rio de Janeiro. Christians must wonder, "What does Christ want for all of the people of that city, and for all of the people of a world that is looking more and more like it?" We must ask. And when we think we know, we must want that, too, and do all we can to bring it to be, because what Christ wants for us is what is really best for us all.[4]

---

1. Joe Hale, Editor, *Proceedings of the Seventeenth World Methodist Conference* (Lake Junaluska, North Carolina: World Methodist Council, 1997).

2. Lester Thurow, "Their World Might Crumble," *New York Times Magazine*, November 6, 1995.

3. Bill Moyers, *Now with Bill Moyers* (PBS Home Video) May 17, 2002.

4. A version of this sermon was originally published in *Pulpit Digest,* September-October, 1998, David Albert Farmer, Editor (Inver Grove Heights, Minnesota: Logos Productions Inc.).

Adam And Evie

Genesis 2:15-17

(A story sermon with dialogical parts that can be read by a pastor and two or more church members.)

Once upon a time, in the first decade of the twenty-first century, the Lord God looked out upon the world and began to reflect upon the long history of interactions that had transpired between God and the human race. It made God tired to think about it. It had demanded so much and it was still not finished. It kept developing new dimensions and each one demanded more and more from God. The Lord thought, "This whole thing has become so complicated. There is so much history involved in it. I wonder what would happen if I should start over at the beginning and do it again. No, I wouldn't want just to cancel out all that I have done. I have too much invested in it. But I wonder if I could start over with a new creation right in the midst of the old one." The Lord God decided to try it.

God took a mass of disorganized energy, pulled it together into a more or less solid state, molded it into a man, and gave it life. God said to the new creature, "I am going to call you Adam. With you, I am going to make a fresh start."

God sought a place on earth as near to the garden of Eden as he could find and he chose an affluent suburban community called Pleasant Grove. There God built a magnificent house with a landscaped garden and a swimming pool. That was to be Adam's home. Near there, toward the center of the city, God built a shiny new supermarket. God gave them both to Adam and said, "Here, I want you to have all of this." Adam looked around and replied:

Adam: That is very nice. Thank you, Lord.

Then the Lord said: "Is there anything else you need?"

Adam: Well, I might get lonely.

So the Lord made Adam a dog to keep him company, man's best friend, a beautiful Airedale.

Adam: He is a beauty, Lord. I am sure that I will enjoy him. But that is not exactly what I had in mind.

The Lord said, "Oh, yes, of course. How could I have forgotten that. Crawl up there in the hammock by the pool and take a nap. When you wake up, I will have a surprise for you."

So Adam took a nap and when he woke up, there was Evie, sunbathing on a chaise lounge beside the pool and smiling at him.

Evie: Hi.

Adam: All right, Lord! Yesss! That is just what I had in mind.

The Lord came and sat down with Adam and Evie and said, "I want to talk to you about your life. You have got it pretty good here. I know you may not understand that since you have never known anything else, but take my word for it, this is good. This is very good. You have much more than most people. I want you to have this. I wish everyone could have this. Now, I want you to be my partner in managing this part of the world. The store will provide a good living for you, but I want you to manage it for me so that it will meet the needs of others as well. Other people will need work and a living. Everyone will need to eat. If you will manage the store like I want you to, it will be a blessing for you and for lots of others as well. Enjoy. Be part of the community. Go to church. Get involved in all kinds of good things. You will be blessed and so will others. There is just one thing I must warn you about. Don't let yourself get too ambitious. If you let yourself get too ambitious, that will mess everything up."

So Adam and Evie lived happily together in their home in Pleasant Grove. They enjoyed life and they enjoyed each other. They worked together to manage the supermarket. The store got a reputation for giving good merchandise at a reasonable price. Happy employees gave courteous service. People came and shopped. Adam and Evie prospered. They also became leaders in the church and community. They were such an attractive couple that everyone liked them. They enjoyed a happy and productive life.

Then one day Evie left the store and went to the bank to make a deposit. When she came out, she noticed a shiny new sports car with dealer's license plates parked next to her car in the parking lot. It was a Ferrari. She let herself walk over to it — and around it. She admired it. She studied the paper tag in the window listing the options and the price. It was quite a car.

Evie: Wow!

Sam: You can have that if you like it.

Evie turned and saw a man in a green blazer standing beside her.

Sam: I am Sam Serpentine from High Status Automotive Imports. That little beauty is for sale and you can have it. The price will be right.

Evie looked at the sticker price and shook her head.

Evie: I don't know ...

Sam: Oh, don't let that sticker price scare you. We can beat that. I know who you are. You can afford this car. I can tell you how. Besides, you deserve it. You and your husband are one of the leading families of the community. You ought to have transportation in keeping with your status. You ought to keep on moving up.

Evie: I don't know. It wouldn't be good for us to get too ambitious.

Sam: Where did you get that crazy idea? Ambition is the motivation that keeps our whole world moving ahead. It makes people work and take risks and venture out. Without ambition, our economy would stagnate and everyone would suffer.

Evie: I never thought of it that way.

The conversation went on for half an hour in the parking lot and for another hour at the dealership and soon Evie pulled up in front of the supermarket in her new car. Sam pulled up right behind her in a second one. One was apple red and the other was fig leaf green — his and hers Ferraris. Evie rushed inside to tell Adam.

Adam came out with a bewildered look on his face, but he was immediately smitten with the shiny new machines.

Adam: How can we afford this?

Evie had an answer all ready.

Evie: There are lots of things we can do to increase our profit. We can stop being so fanatical about quality. We can bump our prices up a little and still be competitive. We can replace some of our people with part-time employees so we will not have to pay so much in employee benefits. There are lots of things we can do.

Adam: But, wouldn't we be being too ambitious?

Evie explained how ambition is the force that keeps the economy from stagnating. Adam let himself be convinced. It really wasn't very hard. Adam jumped into the fig leaf green Ferrari and took it for a spin. Evie followed in her new car. They wound up at the country club where they enjoyed soaking up the admiration of their friends.

After this, things began to change at the store and at the house in Pleasant Grove. Everyone noticed it — except for Adam and Evie.

Then one Sunday morning, Adam and Evie were having brunch by the pool and discussing their plans to buy a condominium in the mountains when the doorbell chimed. Adam could see through the succession of glass walls that the Lord was standing at the front door.

Adam: Oh, my God, it's God. He will want to know why we are not in church. Let's hide. Maybe he will think we are gone.

They both hid in the pool-side shrubs. But the Lord came sauntering up the driveway and saw them.

God: What are you doing in the bushes?

Adam: We were embarrassed because we weren't dressed. That is to say, I suppose we should have been dressed for church by now.

God: Oh. By the way, why aren't you in church?

Adam: Well, to tell you the truth, Lord, we haven't been going to church much any more. They are always talking about antiquated ideas that don't have anything to do with anything that is really important to us. It just doesn't seem worthwhile.

God: Oh? Just what is it that is important to you?

Adam: Increasing our affluence and enjoying it.

God: Oh. Is money really that important to you?

Adam: Sure it is. Money makes the world go around.

God: Oh. I thought there was another explanation for that.

Evie: Lord, what is wrong with being prosperous and having a good life?

God: Nothing. Nothing at all. Don't you remember that I told you I want you to have this good life and I wish everyone else could have this much, too?

Adam: Yes, Lord. We have always remembered that.

God: Do you also remember that I said I want you to be my partner in managing the things you have so that they can bless others as well as you?

Adam: Now that you mention it, I do remember that. But I supposed that you must have been speaking figuratively.

God: Speaking figuratively?

Adam: Yes, speaking figuratively. Surely you know that when you say something that doesn't make sense in terms of the way we usually think about things, we decide that you are just speaking figuratively and we forget it.

God: Oh. Well in plain talk, how are you using your advantages to help others have a good life, too?

Adam: Lord, that is a nice idealistic notion, but you know it will not work. Some people were meant to excel and prosper and other people were meant just to be used by those who excel and prosper.

God: Meant? Meant by whom?

Adam: Meant by ... Well — weren't they?

God: Not that I know of.

Adam: Well ... Okay, forget I said that.

God: Adam, I notice that you two have his and hers Ferraris. Could you be becoming too ambitious?

Adam: It was a gift from my wife.

God: Evie?

Evie: Sam Serpentine sold them to us. He said we deserve them.

Adam: Yes. Besides that, Lord, what is wrong with ambition? What other motivation would make people do their best?

God: What about love?

Adam: Love? What does sex have to do with it?

God: Probably more than you think. But that isn't exactly what I had in mind. How about gratitude?

Adam: Gratitude? I don't owe anybody gratitude. No one has ever given me anything. I have had to work for everything I have ever gotten.

God: Oh!

Adam: What is the matter with you, Lord? You know you can't get your way all of the time.

God: I know. I am the one who decided to make it that way. It just seems that someone would pay attention sometime. I want you to have a good life, but you are about to mess it up. Pretty soon now, things are going to start falling apart for you. Good things will start going sour. I suppose there is no way back for you. I have been down this road before. I know how much you are going to have to go through before you can ever get your life together. And I know how much it is going to cost me to help you do it.

God shook his head sadly and walked off down the driveway. Adam and Evie gave each other a puzzled look.

Adam and Evie: I wonder what he meant by that?

Creative Management Of The Earth

Genesis 2:4-9, 15

God created the earth and the earth was like a beautiful garden full of all of the good things needed to sustain and enrich life. Then God put Adam, our representative in the story, into the garden to "till it and keep it" (Genesis 2:15). That sums up our God-given role in relationship to the world. But how should we keep the earth? How should we manage it? In this day of environmental concerns and environmental crises, that has become a very important question.

Some cynical people have a way of dismissing people who are concerned about the environment as mere nature lovers who can't think of anything bigger than saving the spotted owl, or as modern Druids who are willing to sacrifice people to trees. But, if we take a realistic look at what is happening in our world, we will see that environmental concerns actually have to do with the possibility of the survival and the maintenance of a meaningful quality of life for all future generations of the human race. This is something for which all people, and especially Christians, ought to feel a great responsibility. But that is just the problem — that word, responsibility.

A number of years ago, in an attempt to bring the needs for ecological responsibility to the attention of the people, our country observed the first "Earth Day." The day seemed to have a special relevance to the people of Seabrook, Texas. Seabrook was once a quiet fishing village on the shores of Galveston Bay. It still supports a thriving shrimping industry as well as one of the biggest centers of recreational boating in the country. But, in recent years, Seabrook has also been surrounded by the urban sprawl of the city of Houston, an awesome congregation of petro-chemical industries, and the National Aeronautics and Space Administration's Space center at Clear Lake. All of this has created a number of ecological problems, from the need to protect vulnerable wet lands and to keep green sea turtles from being killed in shrimp nets, to major issues of air and water pollution.

The pastor of the church at Seabrook decided to use Earth Day to bring Christian responsibility for environmental concerns into focus for the congregation. He invited any who were interested or concerned to meet with him to participate in planning the sermon and the service for Earth Day. A significant group of adults and young people were concerned enough to accept the invitation. Among them were some people with valuable expertise and insights. Doug was a marine biologist employed in trying to maintain the health of Galveston Bay and the wet lands around it. Mario was a Navy officer who was both an oceanographer and an astronaut. Bill and Joe were engineers employed in the petro-chemical industry. There were also some other interested young people and adults. The whole group was very aware of the need, the possibilities, and the problems involved in the responsible management of the environment.

Mario said that, as a Navy oceanographer, he has sailed all of the seas of the world and had found the pollution and the floating rubbish resulting from human abuse of the environment everywhere, even in the most unexpected and out of the way places. He also said that he and the other astronauts who look at the earth from space are frequently saddened by seeing the scars left on our earth by deforestation, pollution of the rivers, and other kinds of abuse. He was deeply concerned about all of that.

Doug, the biologist, added that we are using up many of the earth's non-renewable resources and neglecting to renew those that can be renewed. He said that, in the past hundred years, American society has been turned into a vast consuming machine. Joe reflected that an awful lot of people who claim to pay allegiance to a Judeo-Christian religious tradition seem to think that it is our role to conquer the earth and to exploit it rather than to care for it.

Since that first Earth Day, the world has become increasingly aware of the profound effects of the pollution of the atmosphere and the climactic changes that can come from the "green house effect." Global warming could eventually cause such things as the melting of the polar ice cap and consequent rise in the ocean levels. Low lying islands and densely populated river deltas could be flooded. Coral reefs could disappear with the fish that depend upon them. Ecosystems could be drastically altered. The effects of these changes are too complex and threatening to anticipate. We are already seeing the first results of these climactic changes.

Some members of the Seabrook group observed that American businesses seem not to be interested in anything beyond short-term economic gain. And, that is closely related to our society's almost religious commitment to material prosperity and to having more and more. We seem addicted to upward mobility. The reasons for our problems are within us and our chosen lifestyle.

The group observed that if these trends are continued into the future, they could turn our earth into a place that is less and less able to sustain human life, or at least to sustain life of a quality we would want. Some members of the group also asked if we have the right to make the earth untenable for other species, like the African elephant and the great whales.

Things were looking pretty gloomy in the group until Bill injected a more hopeful note. He shared an article he had read that was written by Nobel prize winning microbiologist, Rene Dubos. Dr. Dubos said, "Trends don't have to be regarded as destiny."

Rene Dubos started his work by doing research on the ways in which microscopic organisms first affect their environments and then are affected by them. He expanded those findings into an understanding of how we relate to our environment. We help to form our environment and then our lives are formed by it. He said that the balancing factor is human intelligence. We have the ability to see and understand what is happening and to make decisions about it that will determine what will happen in the future.

This moved the group back to thinking about our Christian understanding of our responsibility for managing the earth. Someone remembered the quotation that said, "Instead of thinking that we have inherited the earth from our ancestors, we should think in terms of having borrowed it from our children."

Our Christian heritage gives us an even better way of thinking about it. It teaches us to think of ourselves having been trusted with the management of the earth by God who is the creator and real owner of it all. The Psalmist wrote, "The earth is the Lord's and all that is in it, the world and those who live in it, for he has founded it on the seas, and established it on the rivers" (Psalm 24:1-2). We are stewards of that which is God's. God put us into this world to till it and to keep it, to manage it. We can understand the concept of management, can't we? We may want to resist the idea that the things we claim to "have" are really God's and not ours, but if we take a long look at things, that is the only understanding that really makes sense. A manager cares for property of another and uses it as the owner wants it used. We know that God wants us to be provided for. The story from Genesis tells us that. But God also wants to provide for everyone as well, including the people of generations yet unborn. What we decide to do with this world will be determined to a great extent by our willingness to be faithful to the purposes of God and by our ability to love our neighbors. Our discussion group quickly began to list the things we can do.

Mike and Amy, the two young people in the group, immediately suggested that we get busy recycling things like paper and plastic and aluminum cans. That is something we can all do. They had the statistics, too. They pointed out that recycling a pile of newspapers four feet high could save a tree by providing the same amount of paper as one tree cut down for pulp wood. Recycling things like plastics and aluminum reduced the amount of non-degradable materials left in our landfills.

Someone else reminded us to buy products that are either made from or packaged in recycled materials. Today's sophisticated marketing techniques tell businesses when people are buying recycled products and that gives them the motivation to keep up the good work.

On a somewhat larger scale, Joe, who is an engineer, observed that industries, especially the petro-chemical industries like those that surround the church, are often presented as the great villains in any consideration of ecological matters. But Joe said he believed that many people in industry are not unwilling to work to save the environment. They will wait to be required to do it so their competition will have to conform to the same standards that limit them. And, they will insist that the requirements be realistic, meaningful, and equitable.

Doug, the biologist, said that scientists have observed that communities of organisms have a way of sensing when they are approaching the limits of their environment's ability to support them and of making necessary adjustments. Clearly, that is what needs to happen now.

There are things that can be done. But that pushes us back to a consideration of the more subtle issues that have to do with our willingness to do them. This moves the issue into the realm of religion, that is to say, into the realm of those deep attitudes and values and commitments that make us do what we do.

The Seabrook group observed that American business and industry too often seems unwilling to think of anything beyond short-term profit. They will use their political clout to resist having any restrictions put on their ability to do business as usual and to exploit the natural resources of the world. That, they observed, is closely related to our culture's almost religious commitment to material prosperity. We seem addicted to upward mobility. The reasons for our problems are within us and our chosen lifestyle. Two recent happenings seem to demonstrate that.

For ten years, the industrialized nations of the world have been working to develop a policy that could do something about global warming. They finally developed the Kyoto (Japan) agreement on how to reduce greenhouse gasses. But our country withdrew from the accord. It is true that there were some problems with the agreement. But it is apparent that we are just not willing to be held accountable to any international agreement that could interfere with business as usual for us. Our country, with four percent of the world's population, produces 25 percent of the world's heat-trapping gasses. Without our participation, little progress can be made.

Shortly after that, in 2002, legislation was presented to the United States Congress that would have required the automobile industry to produce automobiles with greater fuel efficiency and stricter emissions controls. This was suggested partly as a way of reducing dependence on foreign oil and partly to slow the consumption of the world's petroleum resources and to reduce the pollution of the atmosphere. The proposal was defeated. Two reasons were given. The legislators did not want to impose heavy demands upon the automotive industry and, in addition to that, they felt that the American people ought to be able to buy and drive whatever kinds of vehicles they want to. (That year, the number of trucks on the road, including vans and SUVs, had, for the first time, passed the number of automobiles.)

Now, let's reflect on that. Most of us react positively to the idea that we should be able to buy and drive whatever kind of vehicles we want to. We think, "Yeah, it's a free country. I ought to be able to do whatever I want to do!" But is that really right? Can you imagine a family in which one of the children is allowed to do just whatever he wants to do without regard to the needs of the other family members? (Do you remember the story about Harry Potter's spoiled cousin?) That just wouldn't work would it? Neither will it work in the greater family of humankind. We all must learn to live within limitations for the sake of the well-being of the whole family. We have to be willing to have some limitations placed upon our ways of living and doing business so that the environment can be sustained in a condition that can support a good quality of human life for everybody. We have to be willing to accept adult responsibility for that.

Our Christian faith can help us move toward that kind of responsibility. It can set us free from our addiction to upward mobility by giving us a better source of meaning for our lives and a better source of a sense of okay-ness. It can help us to find a better quality of life that does not depend upon always having more and more. It can teach us a commitment that is bigger than our commitment to our own prosperity. It can teach us a commitment to the accomplishment of God's loving purpose for the whole creation. That will give us both the freedom and the motivation to do what really needs to be done to take care of the earth and to use it like God wants it to be used.

In his book, *A God Within*,[1] Rene Dubos, whom we quoted earlier, offers a vision of things as they can be in our world. He suggests that we think in terms of "creative management of the Earth." He says that it is not best to think in terms of "conservation" because ninety percent of the earth's surface has already been profoundly impacted by human occupation and use. And he says that is not necessarily bad. He observes that the land around his home in France had been sustaining human life in a good way for over a thousand years. He also said that we should think in terms, not just of sustaining human life, but in terms of making possible a good and meaningful quality of life. He says that we can take charge of our earth and manage it in creative ways, maybe new ways, to make life possible and good for us and for generations to come. He says this is possible. God calls us to do it.

---

1. Rene Dubos, *A God Within* (New York: Charles Scribner's Sons, 1972).

On Sharing Leadership

Judges 4:1-10

Some of the most far-reaching and conspicuous changes that have occurred in our culture in recent years have been the changes in the roles played by men and women. These changes in gender roles have come about, at least in part, as a result of what has been called "the women's liberation movement." But at its best, the movement should result in a real liberation of both men and women to become all that they can become and to make the best contributions that they can to the society in which they live. Many of us can name the changes we have seen taking place. Most of us are ready to affirm that they are right and good. Some of us feel that we have not yet made all of the changes that need to be made. But there are many of us, both women and men — but especially men — who have not yet completely found ourselves in the new structures of gender roles and relationships. These are very subtle but powerful matters that can have profound impacts upon our understandings of who we are and how we ought to live our lives. If the truth were known, many of us are still struggling to come to terms with the way things are — or perhaps with the way things ought to be.

There is a story in the Bible — really a rather surprising story — that may help us to be able to put things into perspective. It is the story of Deborah.

This story comes from a period that is very far back in the history of the people of Israel, during the period called the time of the Judges. The people had been set free from slavery in Egypt. They had made their journey through the wilderness under the leadership of Moses. Then, under the leadership of Joshua, they had invaded the land of Canaan and settled there. They were progressively forcing out the other people who had lived there. But, there were still fortified cities belonging to certain tribes of the indigenous people. The people of Israel had not yet been united into one nation under a strong king. They lived as scattered tribes who worked together occasionally in times of crisis. The leaders of the people during that time were called Judges. They were emergent leaders whom God raised up when a leader was needed. Time and again during this period, the people of Israel would be seduced into forgetting their covenant with God and slipping into the idolatrous way of the indigenous people. When they did that, they would grow weak and they would be oppressed by their neighbors. Then God would raise up a judge who would call the people back to their covenant with God and lead them against their enemies. The Judges were some of the most colorful heroes in the Old Testament.

Our scripture lesson tells of one judge who was very unique — because she was a woman — Deborah. This was a time when Israel had a patriarchal culture. The men were the ones with status and power. A woman who did not have a man (a father, a husband, a son) to look after her had no legal status and was a very vulnerable person. This is not to say that the women of that age were weak or indecisive. There are lots of Bible stories that demonstrated that they were not. Still, it was very unusual for a woman to hold the position of a judge. But more than that, Deborah was also a prophet, one who spoke for God. Deborah broke all of the rules of traditional gender roles in her day. She was a woman. She had a husband. But she did not stay confined in the traditional role of a wife. She had unique abilities and she used them.

Deborah was judging the people during the time when they were being oppressed by King Jabin the Canaanite, who had a powerful army with 900 chariots of iron commanded by his general, Sisera. The Lord spoke to Deborah and told her that, if the people of Israel would go to fight against Jabin, God would give them the victory. Deborah called Barak, a man who was an able warrior and leader, to mobilize the troops. She was playing a unique role for a woman, but she did not try to make the battle a woman's thing. She had respect for men and called one of them to make his best contribution just as she was making hers. Barak returned the respect. He asked Deborah to go to battle with him. She agreed to do it. They would share the leadership. But Deborah warned Barak that the campaign would not result in his glory because a woman would strike the decisive blow. She was not talking about herself. Barak said that was okay with him. He was not all that interested in glory. He just wanted to free his people from the oppression of the Canaanites. Have you noticed how much better things work out when people are just trying to get a job done instead of competing for glory?

Actually this experiment in shared leadership worked out well. It worked out well for the people of Israel. It worked out well for Deborah. Yes, and it worked out well for Barak, too. He may not have gotten all of the glory that a conquering general usually got. But he certainly came out better than Sisera did. We will talk about Sisera later.

Well, what can we learn from this story?

We can learn that things work out better if everyone is able to become the best and most productive person she or he can become and to make the best contribution that he or she can make instead of being restricted by traditional gender roles. Each of us should be free to become the unique person we are able to be. That, as I understand it, is the message of the liberation movements in a nutshell.

We can also learn that things work out a lot better if, instead of choosing up sides and putting the genders in competition with each other, we can all learn to respect and appreciate each other as unique people with unique abilities and to work together for the good of everyone involved.

And we can learn that we will be much more free to do that if we are mature persons with confidence in ourselves and if we don't feel that we have to prove anything. Then we can concentrate on working to achieve some significant purpose.

Our Christian faith can help us to function in that way because it gives to each of us the affirmation we need to set us free from the need to prove ourselves. It assures us that each of us is a beloved child of God. It also gives us the assurance that each of us has unique gifts to share, a unique personhood to live up to. Our faith also calls us to hold all others in basic respect. And, it gives us a purpose to live for that is great enough to make us willing to subordinate our personal agendas to it.

Now we can use our imaginations to visualize how these principles might work themselves out in our personal lives, in the family, in business, in the church, and in community and government affairs. The implications are very far-reaching and very practical. We should hope for a time when these things are embodied, not just in the social structures of society, but in our personal relationships with one another.

One thing that must be very clear is that liberation that really is liberation is the freedom to be responsible adults, to take charge of our lives, and to manage them responsibly. It is not the freedom to behave like irresponsible children, just to do whatever we want to do without regard for the results of our actions. Some people have very strange ideas about what freedom is.

For instance, a person may choose either to marry or to remain single. But if a person enters into a marriage covenant, there are responsibilities to another person. Two people who choose to marry can design their own lifestyle depending on their own unique needs and abilities. If the woman is the best business person, there is no reason why she should not manage the checkbook. If the man likes to cook, there is no reason why he shouldn't do it. If there are necessary things that neither is good at doing, they should decide together how they are to be done. If a couple decides that each of them will have a career outside of the home, both will have to share the things that need to be done in the home. There is a lot of freedom in that — and it works. It is working for thousands of people.

One thing needs very special attention. Liberated adults must be very careful not to let the needs of their children get lost in their exercise of their freedom. It is unfortunate that, in our excitement about all of the fascinating career opportunities that are open to women, the traditional career of homemaker has often been cast as dreary and unattractive. Women who have chosen that as a full-time vocation have often felt that other women were looking down on them. In fact, it is still one of the most important and demanding careers that anyone could choose.

Whether or not one parent or the other chooses the career of a homemaker, if there are children, there is a responsibility for the children. Children cannot raise themselves. They need the loving commitment and substantial involvement of parents. It ought to be okay for people to choose not to have children. But once there are children, there is a responsibility to work the meeting of their needs into the life of the family. Not to do so is irresponsibility, not liberation. No, the responsibility does not have to belong primarily to the woman. In all families — and especially in two career families — both father and mother should be deeply involved in the lives of the children. That will not just happen by accident, not even in a home with a stay-at-home mom. It takes very intentional planning and action, and it may take the sacrifice of some career advantages. But children have a right to be parented.

Right now, some might want to ask: What is wrong with the old gender roles that were handed down from our grandparents? What is wrong with men opening doors for women and with women being the hostesses in social occasions or with a woman being a "stay-at-home mom"? Of course there is nothing wrong with those traditions. They can be very lovely and fulfilling, provided that they are freely chosen. But when they are forced upon people, either women or men, they can become oppressive and frustrating. Then they can result in the development of some really unhealthy relationships and some really destructive emotions.

Oh, yes, I was going to tell you about Sisera. In the next chapter of the book of Judges, there is a victory song that the people of Israel sang to celebrate their triumph. It mentions the mother of Sisera looking out through the lattice work on her windows and wondering why her son is so long in coming home. Then she comforts herself with the thought that he is surely just going through the spoils to pick out a nice gift for his mother. Suddenly we catch a vision of a man forced into a dangerous and destructive vocation by an ambitious woman who had no way to achieve except through manipulating the men in her life.

When people are not allowed to take control of their lives and to make the decisions that shape them, all kinds of unhealthy and troublesome interactions can develop. And some people who feel forced into roles they haven't chosen can sometimes build up anger that can work either directly or "passively" to hurt others.

Do you know what finally happened to Sisera? When it was apparent to him that the battle was lost, he jumped out of his chariot and hid in the hope of escaping on foot. As he ran, he eventually came to the tent of a Kenite woman named Jael. The Kenites had an alliance of some kind with the Canaanites, so it was not surprising when this properly subservient woman met him and called him "my lord" and invited him to hide in her tent. She brought him a bowl of milk to drink and covered him with a rug. He was exhausted. He fell asleep. And Jael, who had just tucked him in, took a hammer and a tent peg and drove the tent peg all of the way through his skull as he slept. A lifetime of anger and frustration must have gone into that act of violence.

Things work out a lot better for everyone if every person is allowed to take charge of his or her life and to become the person he or she can become without being required to conform to traditional expectations. And things work out better for everyone if we all respect each others' freedom and appreciate each others' unique gifts and work together for the good of all. In doing that, we can find our way to a really healthy kind of liberation for us all.

Weep For The Children

Matthew 2:13-18

Our scripture lesson tells a horror story, innocent children being massacred because of the paranoia of a tyrant. That is a horror story that is still going on. In every age, including our own, the children of the world suffer the most devastating effects of all of the sinfulness of the world. Today's message can't be a happy one. I have to lay on your hearts the suffering of the children of the world. If our humanity is still alive, we will have to join Rachel in weeping for her children. But, hopefully, we will find something more constructive to do than just to weep.

What are we talking about? Where do we find the children of the world suffering because of the sins of the world? Let us count just some of the ways.

When there is war, more children die than soldiers. Many of us still remember the news photograph of a little Vietnamese girl running down a road naked, her face twisted in pain because she had been burned by napalm. But most of the children die in the aftermath of war because the systems needed to care for them have been destroyed. During the war in the Persian Gulf, we systematically destroyed the infrastructure of the enemy nation — the roads, the power plants, the water and sewage systems. It seemed a humane way to wage a war. But in the aftermath, many children were left to be hungry and to get sick and to die. Our country has received a lot of criticism throughout the world for the suffering that is still going on among the children of Iraq. When our country realized what was happening, we made provision for humanitarian aid to get through. But the tyrant found it politically expedient not to allow it. The tyrant never missed a meal. The children are always the victims of war.

When there is famine, the children suffer. A very expressive news photograph came out of a time of famine in Ethiopia. An emaciated child had crumpled and fallen on the way to a feeding station because he did not have the strength to go on, and a vulture was approaching him even though he was not yet dead. This world can still produce enough food to feed all of its residents. But, for reasons that have to have their roots somewhere in human sinfulness, there are still famines. Little children depend on others to feed them. In famines, many children die. And, if a child suffers prolonged malnutrition at certain critical times in its development, it will grow up forever mentally retarded. The children are the most tragic victims of famine.

And children are the victims of poverty. We live in a world where the rich are getting richer and the poor are getting poorer — and more numerous. There are heroic stories of parents who have raised their children to be self-respecting, productive citizens in spite of circumstances of poverty. But it is not easy, and not all parents have the spiritual resources to do that. Poverty prevents many parents from providing their children the opportunities they need to develop to their highest potential. Exhaustion leaves many parents who are struggling to survive without enough energy to give their children the loving care and guidance they need to develop as persons. Child labor is a widespread reality in every part of the world, including ours. Many children of farm laborers have to go to work in the fields at a very early age instead of going to school. In many countries there are laws prohibiting child labor, but authorities are reluctant to enforce them because they know that it is the few cents that the children are able to earn that enable the family to survive. As the children of the poor grow up and see the hopelessness of their situation, it is little wonder that they turn to drug trafficking — or drug use — or other forms of crime for relief. Then we all become victims of their poverty.

Even in our midst, many children suffer child abuse. This is an ugly reality of which we are becoming increasingly aware. We read about it in the newspapers. It happens — and not just on the other side of town. Some children are abused physically. What kind of a person would batter a child? Maybe a very selfish, little-spirited person who resents the demands that the child's needs make upon him or her. Maybe a very desperate person who feels so dependent upon another person who is capable of violence that he or she tolerates the violence. Maybe a very conscientious person, trying so hard to provide for children and care for them under difficult circumstances that exhaustion and frustration push them to a breaking point and rage erupts into violence directed against those whom they actually love.

And there is sexual abuse of children, a thing so ugly that we doubt that we should even mention it in church. A sermon was published by a woman minister, Patricia Ramsden, in which she described the heartbreaking experience of one little girl. She told how the little girl's father would come into her room, speaking softly and assuring her that he would always take care of her and never let anything bad happen to her, then he would rape her violently, then he would go back to assuring her that he would always take care of her. When the child's mother found out what was happening, she called the child all kinds of terrible names, punished her shamefully and withdrew from her emotionally. The description was so graphic that it made the reader very uncomfortable. Then the preacher shared the sad truth that she was describing her own childhood experience.[1] Can you imagine the impact of experiences like that on a child's developing personhood?

And some children are abused emotionally. Some parents, who restrain themselves from abusing their children physically or sexually, still dump on their children verbal abuse — or even worse — subtle abuses that don't correspond to all of the talk about loving relationships.

Compassion requires us to recognize that people who abuse their children are often troubled people. They need help. And we should help if we can. But nothing ever makes it okay for one person to abuse another. We have to join Rachel in weeping for her children.

There is another group of children who suffer the results of our world's sinfulness. This is the category of suffering that may be the largest and the closest to home for us — and the one about which we say the least. These are the children who suffer a special kind of neglect because their parents are too busy pursuing their own personal ambitions, or perhaps trying to give their children the material things our culture values, that they don't have the time or emotional energy left to meet their children's deepest needs for loving relationships. That is a mistake that lots of us have made. In fact, our culture has often encouraged us to make it. The results are sometimes bewilderingly conspicuous, but probably more often subtle and hidden. Our world needs to remember that raising children is a demanding task. It won't be done well unless parents commit themselves to it deeply. And it is one of the most important things a person can do with his or her life. It is worth the effort. All who choose to be parents ought to prepare to make the commitment necessary to do it well. Otherwise, they may have a special kind of experience of weeping for the children.

But is weeping all that we can do? Jesus has shown us how to go beyond weeping. Later in the book of Matthew, there is a story about a time when Jesus was teaching and some parents brought their children for Jesus to bless them. The disciples were about to send them away, saying that Jesus was too busy to be bothered with children. But Jesus said, "Let the little children come to me and do not stop them; for it is to such as these that the kingdom of heaven belongs" (Matthew 19:13-15). Jesus taught us that children are important and that we must make time for them. In another place in Matthew's Gospel, Jesus spoke even more directly. "Whoever welcomes one such child welcomes me. If any of you put a stumbling block before one of these little ones who believes in me, it would be better for you if a great millstone were fastened around your neck and you were drowned in the depths of the sea" (Matthew 18:1-7). Can we identify the millstones that we, as individuals and as a society, are wearing as a result of putting stumbling blocks in the way of our children? Jesus called us all to be child advocates. But in a practical sense, how do we respond to the needs of the suffering children of the world? It is not easy. We cannot always identify the children who are in need. And if we could, we could not always do anything to change their situation — though both law and Christian compassion require us to try. We can, however, work at building a world in which children can find the resources they need to grow up healthy.

We can start by trying to keep ourselves physically and emotionally and spiritually and morally healthy so that we will be capable of loving children, our own children and the children of the world. They need desperately for us to do that.

Then we can intentionally give priority to the needs of children. As we plan our personal lives, and the lives of our families and our churches and our community and our nation and of our world, we can see to it that provision is being made to meet the needs of the children — all of the needs of the children. You would have thought that we could take that for granted, wouldn't you? But evidently we can't.

Then we can create oases of love in the deserts of neglect and abuse where children can come and get their needs met even if they are not being met at home. Certainly, the church should be one such place. Patricia Ramsden, the minister who told about the debilitating abuse she suffered as she was growing up, said that the one place where she was able to find the loving acceptance and affirmation she needed to grow up whole was in the church. In many churches, people frequently have the privilege of participating in the baptisms of children. In some churches, the congregation promises to "so order our lives after the example of Christ that these children, surrounded by steadfast love, may be established in the faith and confirmed and strengthened in the way that leads to life eternal." Something like that is included in many denominations' rituals for infant dedication or infant baptism. When we say that, let's really mean it. It is one of the most important functions of a church.

But it is also important for us to reach out beyond the walls of the church to relate in enabling love to children who may never come into the church. In one community, many caring adults become involved in a program called HOSTS, which means "help one student to succeed." They volunteered to go into the public schools and spend thirty minutes a week tutoring one student who seems destined to fail in school. The tutors came back telling stories of nearly miraculous transformations that had happened in the lives of some of the children just because someone cared enough to pay attention to them. Some of you are probably involved with programs like volunteers in public schools or court-appointed special advocates, or scouting programs or coaching little league. Involvements like that give you opportunities to be agents of God's redemptive love in the lives of children who may have special needs of it, needs of which you may never become aware.

Finally, we must become involved in the politics of love. In a democracy, we the people form public policy and also our nation's foreign policy. Yes, we can still have enough faith in our American system to believe that we do actually influence the decisions that govern our nation. If we really care about the suffering of the children of the world, we must use our influence to shape policies that will provide for the needs of the children of the world. They are the future.

The children of the world are still those who suffer most as a result of the sins of the world. If we care, we will join Rachel in weeping for the children. But if we are committed to the way of Christ, we will go beyond weeping to saying with Jesus, "Let the little children come to me."

---

1. Patricia Ramsden, "For of Such Are the Kingdom of Heaven," *Pulpit Digest*, November-December 1997 (Inver Grove Heights, Minnesota: Logos Productions Inc.), pp. 65-68.

What Will You Do With Your Freedom?

1 Corinthians 8

Once upon a time, there was a happy, moderate church with a friendly, moderate pastor that lived a happy, moderate congregational life that fit in well with the lifestyle of the pleasant community in which it lived. The church members were glad that their church was like that. They told people whom they were inviting to church that they were a happy, moderate church. Sometimes they even thanked God that they were not like some other churches where moralistic preachers delivered long, moralistic sermons condemning smoking and drinking and gambling and other things that were generally accepted in their happy, pleasant community.

As a matter of fact, many if not most of the church members would take a drink now and then. Drinks were served at almost all of the social occasions except for those that were held at the church — though most of the people had forgotten why that was the case. Gambling had recently been legalized and many of the church members were enjoying it as a new hobby. The church members had forgotten, if they had ever known, that the Social Principles of their denomination had anything to say about these things. It had been years since the church had heard a sermon about drinking or gambling, and the members liked it like that.

But the friendly, moderate pastor of the church began to be troubled about that. He heard the state-sponsored lottery numbers being announced on the nightly television news and he heard people talking enthusiastically about their gambling. In one week, six different church members told him about some gambling exploits. One had bought a lottery ticket, two had gone to the next state to a horse race, one had been in a poker game, and two had visited a casino and won. They told him about these things freely because he really was a friendly pastor. But that troubled the pastor because he was counseling with a family that was in the process of disintegrating because the father's addiction to gambling had impoverished them.

The pastor also knew that the dozens of people who came to the church one night a week were coming to attend an Alcoholics Anonymous meeting that was held there. He had attended some of the open meetings and knew the damage and the danger that these people had suffered because of their drinking. He had read the statistics on how many people suffer from alcohol addiction.

It troubled the pastor that the happy, moderate culture of which his church was a part was not only accepting but actually promoting patterns of life that could lead some people into destructive addictions. He decided that it was time to revisit the denomination's forgotten teachings about abstinence.

When the fateful Sunday came, the pastor explained to the congregation that he felt he had to share a message that might not be popular. He said he knew that his might be a minority opinion on the subject. He assured everyone that he respected those whose opinions were different from his and that he did not want to condemn anyone. But, he said, he had a concern he wanted to lay on their hearts. He mentioned that six people had recently told him about their gambling exploits. Of course, he didn't mention their names — but they told him later that he had them worried. Then he preached a sermon about the Christian's responsibility with regard to potentially addictive things like gambling and the use of tobacco and alcohol and other drugs.

The pastor served the church for five years and preached several hundred sermons on many different subjects. But when anyone mentions "the day on which the pastor preached that sermon," everyone knows what is meant.

Friends, it's time for that sermon.

We are people who have claimed our God-given freedom to take charge of our lives and to decide for ourselves what we will do. That is good. But Christian people must make Christian decisions about what we will do with our freedom. People who live in love must consider the impact of their actions on the lives of others. If something is likely to be hurtful to ourselves or to others, love may compel us not to do it.

I suppose we have all been exposed to the kind of religion that is made up mostly of "Thou shalt nots." We don't find it very attractive. And there is a good reason for that. In the final analysis, that is what the Apostle Paul called "life under the law." He said that, ultimately, that is a kind of slavery and that God's love sets us free from it. He urged us to claim our freedom. But he also urged us to use our freedom in love.

Now, perhaps, you can see the relevance of our scripture lesson. Some of you were wondering why in the world we would read a scripture lesson about not eating food offered as a sacrifice to idols. That is not exactly a daily temptation for most of us. But the norm of that teaching applies to many situations that we do encounter daily. Let's dig into this passage.

In the ancient world, in places like Corinth, much of the food, especially the meat, that was offered for sale in the public markets or consumed in public gatherings had been ritually offered as a sacrifice to pagan idols. Most mature Christians did not find that a problem. They knew that God is God and that Jesus is Lord and that an idol is just something carved out of wood and that a T-bone steak is a T-bone steak. They could see no reason for not eating it.

But there were some new Christians in the church at Corinth who had only recently been converted from the worship of idols. For them, the eating of meat that had been offered as a sacrifice to an idol still somehow felt like an act of worshiping an idol. It was a real problem to them. It felt to them like a compromise of their new faith.

Out of loving concern for these new Christians, Paul recommended abstinence from any food that had been offered in worship to other gods. He said, "Take care that this liberty of yours does not somehow become a stumbling block to the weak" (1 Corinthians 8:9). And, for himself, he said, "... if food is a cause for their falling, I will never eat meat, so that I may not cause one of them to fall" (1 Corinthians 8:13).

Now, can you see the relevance of this passage? There are some among us for whom many of the things that are generally accepted in our society are real problems. Loving people ought to be concerned about that.

One of those problem practices is gambling. Our country and our states seem to have gone crazy over gambling. Gambling is sponsored by the states and promoted over our evening television news broadcasts. This is done all in the dubious assumption that gambling revenues will do all kinds of good things that we want done but are not willing to pay for.

In doing this, our culture promotes some very questionable attitudes, like the materialistic value system that tells us nothing could be better than being rich, and the idea that we can get something for nothing.

Some of us are not tempted by gambling. We can't even feel self-righteous about not gambling. If the truth were known, it is not because we are too religious to gamble. It is because we are too tight. We hate to risk losing the money. But for lots of folks, gambling is a real temptation. For many, gambling is an addictive behavior that can take hold of them and destroy their businesses, their families, and their lives. It has been estimated that Americans wager sixty billion dollars a year. Legalized betting costs federal and state governments six billion dollars a year in gambling-related expenses like funding addiction treatment centers and handling a higher number of bankruptcies. Those costs don't include the hardships of families whose bread winner gambled his wages away. The United States Armed Services did a study of 30,000 service men and women and estimated that two percent of them possessed the indicators of probable pathological gambling.[1] It is hard to compute the impact of gambling on our culture, but if we could know its total, I am afraid that it would be staggering.

Have you known some for whom gambling has been a problem? Whether or not you know it, you probably have. How much do you care about them?

The use of tobacco is another practice that is a problem for many. By now, we all know that the use of tobacco is addictive and destructive. Dr. David Kessler says that 2.8 million people die every year, worldwide, as a result of the use of tobacco.[2] Some of us have seen a dramatic change in the attitude of the country toward tobacco in our lifetime. The use of tobacco is declining. But 3,000 children in the United States start smoking every day and one out of three of these will eventually die from their smoking, according to Dr. Kessler. See how hard it is for us to reject anything that is as profitable as the tobacco industry just because it is destructive to human life? That says something awful about our culture's value system.

A certain high school guidance counselor was active in the state war against drugs. He has become an expert on the subject. He said something that is really frightening. He said, it will be very hard to finally defeat the drug trade because there is so much money in it. If the total dollar value of the drug trade in our country could be known, it would probably be one of our biggest businesses, if not the biggest. And in a country where money controls everything, the drug trade will be awfully hard to defeat.

Now we need to talk about alcohol. Do we hear lots of you saying, "No, let's don't"? But we really need to. For many of you, drinking alcoholic beverages has become a part of your life. How important a part of your life has it become?

We all know, don't we, that alcohol is potentially addictive and destructive?

Alcoholism is a huge problem among us. Some have estimated that one in every eight adult Americans is a potential alcoholic. That means that one person in eight is a person who, if he or she begins to drink with any regularity, will develop the addictive patterns of alcoholism. They will not be able to drink at all without drinking to excess. Compulsive drinking can destroy businesses, families, and lives even more completely than can gambling. This is a problem for lots of people. In every community across the country, several nights a week, thousands of people attend meetings of twelve-step programs to get help in coping with alcoholism. Those who do that are getting help and getting their lives together again. An awful lot of people are not getting help. Alcoholism is a huge problem for a huge number of people — and there is no way of knowing whether or not you are a potential alcoholic until the patterns of addiction begin to emerge.

But that is only one of the ways in which alcohol can destroy people. Every year, thousands of people die in traffic accidents that are the result of someone driving while intoxicated. An epidemic of binge drinking is sweeping our college campuses and causing the deaths of many bright young people and interfering with the lives and educations of many others. Thousands of people also die as the result of the physical harm alcohol can do to their bodies — liver damage, lung cancer that has spread to the brain, and others. Friends, if you have ever seen that happen to someone whom you have loved and admired, you will know that it is a heartbreaking thing. God doesn't want that to happen to you.

The use of beverage alcohol is more closely related to other forms of drug abuse than we want to think. It is really very hard to compose a definition of a drug that does not include tobacco and alcohol unless you make a distinction between legal and illegal drugs. Our young people see that relationship very clearly. We love our young people and we want nothing but the best for them, yet many of us set examples that can lead young people into excessive drinking, binge drinking, and other forms of drug abuse. We really need to think hard about that.

Can you see that we have allowed our culture to develop some patterns of life that are very dangerous for many people? How many of you have ever been in a social or business situation where it would have been hard for you not to participate in the gambling or drinking or other kinds of potentially addictive behavior that everyone seemed to be doing? Can you imagine what it would be like to be in that situation if you knew that you were someone who could become addicted? Worse, can you imagine what it would be like to be in one of those situations and not know that you were someone who could become addicted?

Now can you see why many churches recommend abstinence? Abstinence is not about self-righteous superiority. Abstinence is about loving concern.

Healthy self-love is one reason for leaving potentially addictive things alone. If you knew that there was only a one-in-eight chance that a rattlesnake would bite you, would you play with rattlesnakes? Someone once said to a pastor, "Preacher, I don't think I am a bad person for taking a little to drink." The pastor responded that the point is not that you are bad, but that you are good. You are a good and beautiful creature of God, someone whom God loves. God wants you not to do things that could hurt you. God wants something better for you than those things might do to you. And I want something better for you and for everyone else, too.

Many Christians have become convinced that love for others who might be led into self-destructive addictions requires them not to gamble or to use tobacco or alcohol or other drugs. Wouldn't it be easier for those people if there were some people who would live so that "Everybody is doing it" would not be true? Think hard about that. Love requires us to live in a way that will not influence others to do things that are hurtful to them. If you won't become an abstainer, at least learn how to give a party that will not put your guests under pressure to drink or to do other things that could be hurtful to them. Think about that. It is a matter of Christian caring.

Finally, seek and find other ways to make life full and good and to live it joyfully and share that with your friends. That is something awfully important. We will never be able to stop the drug traffic and all of the corrupting and criminal activity that goes with it by cutting off the supply. As long as there is a demand, there will be a supply. Our best hope for putting an end to all of the drug-related problems of our society is for more and more people to know how to live full and satisfying lives without drugs. The same can be said of other forms of potentially addictive behavior. Claim the gift of fullness of life that God offers to us and share that with your friends. That is what real love will make us want to do.

Well, you can relax now. This sermon is over. We really needed to say what was said and now it has been said. It's over. Yes, you are free to do whatever you choose to do about it. But what will you do with your freedom? Will you use it in love?

1. Joshua Kurlantzick, "Gambling's Royal Flush," in *U.S. News and World Report* (New York: U.S. News and World Report, Inc.) May 20, 2002.

2. David Kessler, *A Question of Intent: A Great American Battle with a Deadly Industry* quoted by Philip E. Beal in "Tobacco Holocaust Grows" in *The United Methodist Reporter* (Dallas, Texas: United Methodist Communications Inc.), May 31, 2002.

Feeding God's Sheep

John 21:15-17

"If you love me, feed my sheep." These words that Jesus spoke to Peter, and to us, make it clear that, if we really love Jesus, we will show it by ministering to the needs of the people whom Jesus loves. In fact, those who love Jesus find it natural to want to respond to the needs of others. An awful lot of people who love Jesus have been wishing lately that they could find effective ways of ministering to the needs of children and youth in our families and in our communities. We have all been made heartsick by the reports of violence in Columbine High School in Littleton, Colorado, and of the other similar eruptions of violence. We have been saddened by reports of young people committing suicide and of other evidences of anger and desperation among the young people whom we love, the ones upon whom we always hang our hopes. One older man spoke for us all. He had been confined to the hospital for a time and was compelled to watch the reports of the news from Littleton day by day on television. He said, "I feel so helpless. I wish there were something I could do."

There is something we can do. We can feed God's sheep.

We are all familiar with the recent events that have called forth a nationwide response of loving anxiety about our children and young people. Growing up has never been easy. But evidently the stresses and failures of contemporary culture are making it more difficult than ever. But, before we plunge into involvement, we will do well to remember certain things about the situation we are addressing.

The stresses and failures of contemporary culture may be making it harder for young people to grow up healthy than it was in some situations in the past. But the difficulties are not entirely new. It is not just in recent years that youthful frustrations have turned into anger and been vented in destructive ways against friends and family members. Do you remember a story about two boys named Cain and Abel? (Genesis 4:1-16). Frustration and anger and jealousy and violence have been around so long that they are frequently represented in those early biblical narratives that were intended to teach us about the basic shape of life in human society.

It is also terribly important to remember that not all young people are afflicted with the maladies we hear so much about. Destructive forces are at work in the society of children and young people, but the living God is at work there, too. Do you remember that in one of the earlier school shootings, some of the high school boys risked their lives in a very heroic way to wrestle the gun from the hand of the shooter? Do you remember that, in the Columbine High School tragedy, one young girl was asked if she believed in God and she sacrificed her life rather than deny her faith? That kind of commitment reminds us of the faith of the early Christian martyrs. In one of the schools in one city where there have been suicides, there is a group of students who, with the assistance of their teachers, are trying to offer hope and help to students who feel drawn toward suicide. When we think about what needs to be done for children and youth today, it is very important not to think about working *on* our kids and trying to fix them. It is important to think in terms of working *with* our young people and children, knowing that God is already at work among them and that there is much in each young person and in each group of young people that is working hard to move toward a life that really is truly human and deeply good.

That is not to say there is nothing to worry about. Day by day, the decision is still being made between life and death, between blessing and curse (Deuteronomy 30:19). The intensity of the struggle and the difficulty of the decision are really great today. If we care — if we love Jesus — we will certainly feel called to get involved.

But the situation is not simple and the solutions will not be easy. Just putting prayer back in public schools will not solve the problem. One of our schools where teens are troubled is not a public school. It is a parochial school. Prayer is offered there daily.

Just wiping out poverty will not solve the problem. Surely you have noticed that the schools in the news lately have been the schools of the affluent. Just hiring youth directors and building gymnasiums in all of the churches will not solve the problem. Neither will anything else that you can do with a checkbook alone.

And sometimes, even if you really give yourself in love to your children and do all of the right things, things still will not turn out right. A group of church people had an opportunity to visit with a greatly admired former pastor. They heard him tell, with great courage and with tears, how he and his wife had done everything they knew to do to lead their daughter into life at its best. But she seemed determined to follow the way of the drug culture. They kept on trying, reaching out to her in love, paying for drug rehabilitation programs, doing all they knew to do. But in spite of it all, in her young adulthood their daughter took her own life. There are no easy answers and there are no guaranteed results.

But there is still the call of Christ, "If you love me, feed my sheep."

How can we do that? A pastor met a man wearing a t-shirt with the letters P.L.A.Y. written on it in bright colors. Under the initials were the words, "Participate in the life of American youth." He said it was just something he believes in. He had the right idea. We have to become participants in that struggle between life and death, blessing and curse that is always going on in the lives of children and young people and their culture. Well, how, then, can we do that?

Obviously, there are some changes that could be made in our culture that would make it more healthy. Violence in the entertainment media is not a healthy thing. Movies and video games that invite young people to picture themselves as heroes who wade into the midst of crowds of "enemies" with weapons blazing leaving piles of dead bodies behind cannot be good for anyone. It should not surprise us that some troubled kids would eventually act out those roles in tragic ways. The ready availability of firearms, even assault weapons, the exploitation of sexuality, and the general acceptance of the use of alcohol and other drugs are other dangerous conditions that we should try to change if we can.

At a much deeper level, there are basic spiritual problems that need to be addressed in our culture. Our actions do not always match our professed beliefs. A lifestyle that consistently puts material values above human values is the most conspicuous example of that. We can see that most clearly in the lives of parents who think the best thing they can do for their children is to work all of the time to give their children the advantages of affluence, even if that means not having time to spend in building relationships with them. Children and young people have an uncanny ability to pick up on these inconsistencies. Our little and big adult hypocrisies do not go unnoticed. They undermine the ability of young people to have confidence in anything. Our children and young people need for us and our adult society to repent of a lot of things most of us are not ready to repent of yet and to live lives of attractive integrity. That is a tall order, isn't it? We asked what we can do.

The most important thing we can do — and it is something that we *can* do — is to open ourselves to the children and young people around us and to build important, helpful relationships with all who will let us. This is most important, of course, in our relationships with our own children. But it is also important for us to build relationships with our stepchildren, grandchildren, nieces and nephews, the neighbors' kids, and any other kids that come within reach. If you want to rise to a really high calling, get involved in the youth ministry of your church or as an adult worker with a scouting or athletic program or as a tutor in a school. You will not have to look far to find an opportunity to do that.

Relationships with children and young people can be a real joy. But sometimes they can become difficult and painful. When those times come, hang in there. Don't withdraw. Those painful interactions may be parts of the transactions that are shaping a life. At times, your own children may seem to want you to get out of their lives. When that happens, withdraw enough to give them the space they need to become separate persons — but don't go away. They need for you to set limits and give their lives structure. They need for you to be there for them when they need you. And they will need for you to move back into their lives in somewhat altered but still very important roles after they have accomplished their growing tasks. Building important, helping relationships with young people is the most important thing you can do for them and, whether or not it is apparent, it is what they want you to do for them.

Then what should we do with those relationships? Our first inclination is to use them to tell the young people all that we have learned in life and then to tell them what they ought to do. There will be a time for that. But the first thing we need to do is to listen to the children and young people. Let them tell you who they are, how they feel, and what is going on in their lives. Don't pry. Just wait and listen. It will come out. Then tell them what is right with them. Affirm everything you can find to affirm about them. Help them to build up the personhood that is developing in them. There will be a time for you to share your life experiences with them. But wait for the time when they are ready to hear it. Then share it simply as your story, not as the model for what they should do. In the same way, look for opportunities to share your religious faith with them. Do it simply, without trying to push it on them. Let them know what is real and important and helpful to you. That kind of witness will have its effect if it takes place within a real, caring relationship.

There is no guarantee that these things will produce any particular result. The young person's future will ultimately be in his or her hands. But you can be a valuable friend if you will simply move into a relationship and go where the young person's real needs lead you.

What we have said about how adults can be helpful in their relationships with young people also applies to the relationships of young people with other young people. You know how important your interactions with your peer groups are. Try to be helpful to one another. Try to build one another up. One of the tragic aspects of the Columbine High story is that it showed how angry some young people are at the other young people who have rejected them or "put them down." Young people need both adult friends and young ones — and the need is urgent.

All of this is a way of saying, "Love your neighbors, especially the young ones." We all need loving relationships. Suicides and attempted suicides are often cries for loving relationships. Acts of violence are often protests against the absence of loving relationships. Children and young people, perhaps more than the rest of us, are hungry for that kind of relationship. If they receive love, they may thrive and grow. If they don't, they may wither and die, either spiritually or physically, and they may drag others into death with them. There is a deep hunger there. Remember what Jesus said, "If you love me, feed my sheep."

Thinking About Suicide

Psalm 130

One day several years ago, a pastor was called by a church member and asked to visit one of his neighbors in whose home a tragedy had just happened. The neighbor's teenage son had used a rifle from a family gun collection to end his own life. The family was distraught and they had asked to talk to a minister. The pastor arrived less than an hour after the suicide happened. The family told him the whole heartbreaking story about family troubles, a young person who just couldn't seem to get his life together, a trivial conflict that triggered a terrible reaction, and the emotional devastation that the whole family was experiencing. The family joined the church and the pastor became their friend and worked with them during the following months to help them work through all of the problems and issues that came in the aftermath of that tragedy. They believed that the Christian faith had something to offer to people who are trying to cope with suicide. Indeed it does.

Our faith has important and helpful things to say to communities in which suicide happens, to families and friends of people who have committed suicide, and to people who may secretly be thinking of suicide as a way of ending their own lives. Every now and again, suicide pushes itself into our lives, and we find ourselves thinking about suicide. Let's think about it for a while in the light of the Christian faith.

It is hard for most of us to imagine what would make a person commit suicide. Yet, many people do not find it unthinkable. It is the second largest cause of death among teenagers in our country. And depression, the emotional condition which leads many to commit suicide, is widespread among people of all ages.

Suicide is a tragedy that happens when people lose hope. Suicide beckons to some people when they have lost all self-esteem, when they feel alone and not close to anyone who can help, when life is experienced as being "not good" and when there is no visible reason to hope that it will get better, when the problems of life seem overwhelming and there is nothing apparent that could solve them. Under circumstances like that, some may eventually begin to think that suicide would be a solution.

What does the Christian faith say about suicide? We have heard that many Christians believe that a person who commits suicide cannot hope to go to heaven because he or she has committed a sin for which he or she will have no opportunity to ask to be forgiven. But that imposes a very legalistic structure on a situation that is very complex. Our hope for heaven depends, not on our own rightness, but upon God's mercy. God, whose mercy reaches out past so many of our failures, can surely reach out past one act done in desperation, and deal with the whole person.

Well, what does the Bible say about suicide? Surprisingly, very little. From history, we know that suicides did happen in biblical days. But the Bible doesn't say much about it.

The Bible does, however, say lots of things that are relevant to people thinking about suicide. It tells us that God loves us with a great and perfect love, that God accepts us and forgives us, that God values us as precious children of God. The Bible tells us that life is a good gift from God and that God wants us to receive it gratefully and live it fully. The Bible tells us that God is at work in our lives and in the history of our world, often in ways that we cannot see or know, and that God is at work in all of those ways to save us from our troubles and to help us make life good. And the Bible tells us that God wants us to love one another and to do what we can to help each other make life good. All of these basic affirmations of the Bible have a lot to say to anyone who is thinking about suicide.

Even though the Bible says very little about suicide, it says a great deal about desperation and despair. The psalm we read as our text is one of a type of psalms that is often found in the Bible. It is the prayer of someone who is in trouble. "Out of the depths have I cried to you, O Lord." The psalmist then goes on to remember that God has been there to help his people in their times of trouble down through the years. In faith and expectancy, the person praying turns to the invisible God who often works in ways beyond our understanding, and asks for help. That is an approach to trouble that can be very helpful to anyone who is thinking about suicide.

What does our faith have to say to communities in which suicides happen? Paul reminds us that the decisions we make help to create the environment in which others live, and he urges us to make our decisions, not insisting upon our own rights but rather in loving concern for our neighbors. One of the big issues in the church in Paul's day had to do with whether the early Christians should eat meat that had been offered to idols. Paul said that there is really nothing wrong with eating meat but, because it was causing real spiritual problems for some recent converts from idol worship, he would abstain from eating meat. He said, "... it is good not to eat meat or drink wine or do anything that makes your brother or sister stumble" (Romans 14:21). In another place, he said, "For you were called to freedom, brothers and sisters, only do not use your freedom as an opportunity for self-indulgence, but through love become slaves to one another. For the whole law is summed up in one commandment, 'You shall love your neighbor as yourself' " (Galatians 5:13-14). By following that rule, we may actually save the lives of some who are in danger of suicide.

There are lots of people who have very low self-esteem. We should learn to relate ourselves to every person in a way that affirms and evokes his or her own dignity as a person. Some of us, especially men and young people, practice a kind of humor that cuts other people down. We don't mean anything by it. But our cutting humor hurts. And we have developed a way of evaluating persons' lives that recognizes only one way to be a success. Those who can't be winners in that game must always think of themselves as failures. All of that is dangerous to people with a tenuous hold on the will to live. Could we change that?

And we need to think seriously about the social customs that set traps for people who are at risk. For instance, we need to think seriously about our love for the use of alcohol and other drugs. A high school conducted an assembly to help young people cope with the recent suicide of a fellow student. There were several speakers. The students heard each one appreciatively and responded with affirming applause. Then the school counselor spoke and reckoned with the fact that the student had been intoxicated when he took his life. He ended by saying, "Alcohol is killing us." The applause of the students was about half what it had been for the other speakers. They were communicating an ambivalence which reflects the ambivalence of our society as a whole. We know that alcohol and other drugs are killing people. But we are not willing to give them up as a part of our lives. Love requires us to reckon with that.

Finally, we need to be sensitive and responsive to the needs of others around us. There are lots of troubled people who need someone to talk to. We always seem to be too busy for each other, even for those who are closest to us. We need to find ways of being available to listen to each other when someone really needs to talk. And when someone communicates to us that he or she is deeply troubled, especially if there are thoughts about suicide, we need to take those needs seriously and help the person find the help that is needed.

Our world is often harsh and demanding and indifferent to our hurting. It is probably unrealistic to say that we need to change all of that about our world. But we can create little clearings of compassion in the forest of hurtfulness where people in trouble can find affirmation and help.

What does the Christian faith have to say to someone who has lost a friend or family member to suicide? Pretty much the same thing it has to say to anyone who has lost a loved one to any tragic death. We have already said that it is not necessary to think that a person who has ended his or her own life as a person cannot be saved. There are many premature or accidental deaths that crash into the lives of families and communities and are devastating in very similar ways. Think of suicide as one of these.

Of course, that will by no means make the death easy to deal with. Tragic deaths often fill the lives of friends and family members with great storms of guilt and anger and grief and all sorts of other experiences that are hard to explain.

If there are feelings of guilt making us wonder if there was something we could have done to prevent the suicide, we will need to deal with that. If, in fact, you could have done more, and we usually could have, then repent of that shortcoming and resolve to be a more responsive person. But know that we all fall short and we all need God's saving grace to enable us to accept ourselves so that we can take up our lives and live them on into the future. Remember, you are not the one who decided to end your friend's life. He or she did. It will be important for you to pull your own life together with the help of God.

Anger may be another part of the experience. You may be angry at the one who committed suicide, angry at yourself for not being able to prevent it, angry at God for letting it happen. Anger can be a healthy emotion. It cries out, "This was wrong." Own your anger. But keep it in perspective. Deal with it until you can forgive yourself and your friend — and God. Deal with it until you can accept the fact that, wrong as it was, the suicide happened. Assimilate it into your lifetime of experiences and move ahead, having learned from it.

Of course grief is a part of the experience of losing someone you love. There is a big empty spot. Life has to be reorganized without one who once was part of it. The Christian's faith in the resurrection can always help us deal with grief. It is no different in the case of a loss by suicide. Entrust your loved one to God who loves us all and trust God's promise to receive and to raise those whom he loves up to new life beyond this life. And entrust yourself, too, to the risen Christ, who is at work in our lives, in the hope that you, too, will eventually be raised up out of guilt and anger and grief and all of the other bewildering things you may be experiencing and that you will be given back your life so that you can live fully again.

Finally, we have to ask, what does the Christian faith have to say to those who may be thinking about committing suicide? What does it give us to hold on to when our lives seem to darken into gloom and we begin to think that the best thing we can do is to end our lives?

Our Christian faith tells us that God loves us, even when we can't love ourselves, and that our lives are precious to God, even if they seem, for a time, not to be precious to us. It tells us that God has given us our lives as good gifts and that God wants our lives to be good and that God is working to make our lives good, even if we cannot see that. It tells us that even when our lives are terribly messed up and we cannot see any way for them to be put right again, there is one whom we can't see who is at work to save. Remember those things and, if you ever find yourself thinking about suicide, talk to yourself about them.

While you are talking to yourself, talk back to those sinister voices that talk nonsense from the dark corners of your mind. Don't let yourself get enamored with the idea of suicide as if there is something glamorous or heroic about it. There is nothing glamorous about it. In most cases, it is terrible. And it is not heroic. There is all of the difference in the world between going to meet your death with courage when it is time to die on the one hand, and using death as a way to escape from the difficulties of life on the other. And don't let yourself be seduced into thinking that your suicide will solve problems that you have caused in the lives of people you love. Far from solving problems, your suicide would create more problems than you can imagine for the ones you love. The stepfather of a young man who had committed suicide told his classmates, "If you think this world will be a better place without you, forget it. This world will not be a better place without you!" And don't try to escape into alcohol or other drugs. They will only deepen your depression and take away what good judgment you have left.

Hold on tightly to the good gift of life and believe that, because God is a living God, there is always hope for you. Then look for the ways in which God may be reaching out to help you. Much depression may actually be the result of chemical imbalances in our bodies, and medical care can be the agent of God's saving work. Go to see a doctor. If the problems are more complex than that, then sharing your feelings with a caring friend can help you to get things into perspective. Find someone who is willing to listen to you. Keep looking until you find someone who will take your hand and help you climb out of the gloom. If you need to, get psychiatric help. Forget the stigma. This is your life we are talking about. Even if you can't see how your problems could ever be solved, know that there is one who is at work to help in your life in ways that you cannot know or anticipate. Put your trust in God and God will give you back your future.

Resurrections still happen. One of the most prominent preachers in our country witnessed to an experience of saving grace. He told about a time when he had sunk so deep into depression that the only thing that kept him from taking his own life was that he didn't want his children to remember that their father had been both a minister and a suicide. Finally, he checked himself into a hospital for psychiatric treatment. He said that healing did not come soon or easily. But finally, a great light came into his darkness and led him back to life. That was his way of describing what happened to him. He was able to pick up his life again and to live it fully, joyfully, and fruitfully and to be an effective servant of the Lord for many years. Resurrection can happen to you, too.

Take the words of the psalmist for your prayer and discover the hope into which they have led people for thousands of years. "Out of the depths have I cried to you, O Lord. Lord hear my voice ... There is forgiveness with you ... I wait for the Lord, my soul waits and in his word I hope; my soul waits for the Lord more than those who watch for the morning, more than those who watch for the morning." Hold on to your life and trust God to make it better. If you hold on to it, your life can get better. If you let it go, it can't. Hold on and wait for the morning.

The Radicalizing Of Charlie

Amos 5:14-15

(*A sermon in the form of a chancel drama.*)

Narrator: These words from the prophet Amos remind us that Christians are called to make a difference in society. The Church is called to be the representative of morality and human dignity, to serve as the conscience of the community, to be a change agent, to act decisively in the service of all that is true and just and good. But it is not always easy to know how to do that. Can the Church be decisive and influential in society without being radicalized and becoming part of the polarization that tears society apart? Today we are going to watch a dramatization that raises that question. It is intended to raise questions, not to answer them. When it is over, you will have to do some of the hard work of decision making that is part of Christian decisiveness. The drama begins in a pastor's study. The door stands open as it usually does. Charlie is just arriving to keep an appointment with the pastor.

Charlie: Hello, pastor. Do you have time to talk with me?

Pastor: Sure, Charlie. I have been expecting you. Come on in. I have some fresh coffee.

(*The two men pour cups of coffee from a thermos and sit down in chairs facing each other.*)

Charlie: You are not going to like what I am going to tell you. I have decided that I have to leave this church.

Pastor: I was afraid you were going to say that.

Charlie: I know that you know why. I just can't tolerate this church's ambivalence on the issue of abortion. After all of our conversations about this, I know it won't come as a surprise to you.

Pastor: No, I am not surprised. I know how strongly you feel about it.

Charlie: I feel that legalized abortion is an evil of unspeakable magnitude. More than a million innocent babies a year are being murdered before they are born.[1] I can't imagine why this church does not take to the streets crying out in protest.

Pastor: I understand how you feel.

Charlie: I can't understand how you can tolerate this ambivalence. If you really believe some of the things I have heard you say, I can't understand why you are not feeling just as I do.

Pastor: Charlie, as I have told you, this church doesn't believe in abortion and neither do I. We do believe that abortion is the termination of a human life. It makes me sick to think that it is sometimes done irresponsibly, just to avoid embarrassment or inconvenience. But there is another side to the issue. In real life, there are lots of ambiguous situations. There are situations in which the needs of one life must be weighed against the needs of another life. There are a few tragic situations in which an abortion may be the lesser of two evils. I have known of some situations in which people chose to have an abortion and the circumstances were such that I could not bring myself to say they were wrong. I really don't think the church is being ambivalent. I think it is just trying to be realistic.

Charlie: I can't see that. There are not that many cases in which a pregnancy threatens the life of a mother. Everyone talks about cases of rape and incest. Even in these cases you are talking about balancing one person's suffering against another person's existence.

Shouldn't people be willing to endure suffering to preserve the life of another?

Pastor: I think it is a heroic thing when someone decides to do that, but it is hard to sit on the sidelines and make that kind of a decision for another.

Charlie: Doesn't all moral teaching tell people how they ought to decide?

Pastor: No, some helps people to work out their own decisions.

Charlie: You know it is not as if the mothers are being asked to keep the children and raise them. If they will just let them live, there are others who will adopt them and raise them.

Pastor: Yes, I believe that, as they say, "Adoption is the loving option." Our church has been supporting a home for unwed mothers and licensed adoption agency for 100 years.

Charlie: But, pastor, what we are talking about right now is a small minority of the cases of abortion. What is actually happening in the real world is not that abortion is being used to resolve tragic conflict between lives. What is actually happening is that thousands of babies are being killed so that people can keep up an irresponsible and self-indulgent lifestyle.

Pastor: I have a sick feeling that you may be right about that.

Charlie: And, if the church just stands around worrying about the tragic exceptions, it will become completely indecisive in the shaping of public morality.

Pastor: Not necessarily. We can always urge people to make moral decisions. Letting something be legal is not the same as saying it is morally right. Christians have always made loving decisions that required them to go beyond the requirements of secular law.

Charlie: I will give you credit for preaching that. But to stand by and let something be legal that is so totally immoral sends a mixed signal. The vast majority of people believe that if something is legal it is okay.

Pastor: Charlie, you are expressing a pretty negative attitude toward public morality.

Charlie: I am just being realistic. You know that I have not always been a Christian. You can remember what I was like six years ago when I first came to this church. I know how people in this world think and feel and act. I used to be part of it. I lived just like they are living until I saw that it was leading me to a dead end.

Pastor: Yes, I remember.

Charlie: I know how people think. They never give a thought to what is right. They just think about what serves their own selfish interests.

Pastor: Charlie, be careful not to read your own worst motives into the decisions of others. You eventually came around to a different way of life, didn't you?

Charlie: Yes, but there was so much damage done before I did.

Pastor: Damage?

Charlie: (*Pauses, then goes on hesitantly.*) Yes, damage. (*Stands, looks away, takes a few steps away and goes on talking while looking away.*) There is something I have never told you. It is too painful to talk about. Before I became a Christian, I once got a girl pregnant. I paid for her to get an abortion. She would have had the baby if I had encouraged her to, but I didn't want any part of that. I was only interested in pleasure and I only wanted the easiest way out of a problem situation. I know how people think.

Pastor: I know that must be a tremendous burden to you, Charlie.

Charlie: It really is. I never wanted to talk about it. I still have a hard time dealing with it.

Pastor: Charlie, the Christian faith has a way of helping us to deal with things like that. It has to do with the forgiving love of God. It can help you get free from your guilt.

Charlie: But it can't undo the fact that I made that girl kill our baby.

Pastor: Charlie, is there any chance that the reason you feel so strongly about this issue is that you feel that you have to do something to atone for your guilt?

Charlie: I don't know. Maybe.

Pastor: If that is true, Charlie, be careful. If you let guilt drive your life, it may drive you to do some things that really don't need to be done.

Charlie: What do you mean?

Pastor: Sometimes guilt drives us to punish ourselves and to punish others whom we perceive to be like ourselves.

Charlie: Is that wrong?

Pastor: It can be dangerous. Guilt is not a healthy motive for anything but repentance. It is a lot like hate — self-hate. It is a lot better to claim the freedom God offers to us through his forgiving love and then let our actions be formed by healthier motives and by clearer visions. It is better to do what needs to be done than to do what we need to do.

Charlie: I'll think about that.

Pastor: Do. It's important.

Charlie: (*Sits down again and faces the pastor.*) You know, pastor, I have to admit there is an inconsistency in what I am doing. The very thing that is driving me out of this church is the thing that once drew me into it.

Pastor: What's that, Charlie?

Charlie: Acceptance. The willingness not to condemn. The willingness to take people as they are and to believe the best about them and to try to love them into being something better. When I first came to this church six years ago, I was a dirty, immoral, drug-using failure. I realized that my life was at a dead end. I came to this church fully expecting to be rejected. I came to let you reject me so I could feel justified in committing suicide. That really was my plan. But this church didn't reject me. You accepted me as I was and loved me into hoping things could be better. Pastor, your sermons helped me find a better way of life. I will always love this church for that. I met Judy here in this church. We were married here. Our baby was baptized here. I will always love this church. Leaving it is one of the hardest things I ever had to do.

Pastor: We will always be here for you if you ever feel that you can come back.

Charlie: Somehow I knew that. But, thanks for saying it. Say, by the way, did you get to look at the videotape I left for you.

Pastor: Yes.

Charlie: What did you think of it.

Pastor: Well, there were some good things in it, but it was awfully emotional in its condemnations. All of those comparisons of legalized abortions to the Nazi extermination of the Jews will seem a little extreme to most people. I am afraid it is more like a war dance to whip up the anger of those who agree with it than an argument that would convince those who don't.

Charlie: Well, isn't the wholesale killing of unborn babies like the holocaust? Isn't it like the slaughter of the innocent? As far as I am concerned, the people who kill babies are murderers and ought to be treated like murderers. Someone has to stop them from killing innocent babies.

Pastor: Charlie, I hear you almost saying something now that really scares me. There are people in the pro-life movement who have actually committed assassinations. You are not saying you believe in that, are you?

Charlie: No. No, not really. The point is to stop the killing. But still, I remember that the church has made a hero of Dietrich Bonhoeffer who was implicated in a plot to assassinate Hitler. I can understand why some people feel compelled to take radical action to stop the killing.

Pastor: Charlie, I am worried about that. Where will you go when you leave this church? Will you join another church?

Charlie: Yes, I will join one of the churches that has taken to the streets in protest against the killing. I will get more involved in the movement.

Pastor: Charlie, be careful not to get so completely involved in this movement that you are surrounded by people who are all saying the same thing. We all need to hear the other side of things. We need reality checks. Bad things happen when people get so caught up in an issue that they identify those with whom they disagree as enemies. They sometimes treat them like things to be gotten rid of rather than as people to be understood.

Charlie: I have heard the other side of things from you. I won't forget.

Pastor: By the way, will Judy be transferring her membership, too?

Charlie: (*Pauses and looks down.*) No. No, pastor. Judy and I are separating. We still love each other, but Judy thinks I have gone off the deep end. She just doesn't feel that she can go with me where I feel that I have to go.

Pastor: Oh, Charlie, I am really sorry to hear that. You are really paying a high price for following your convictions, aren't you?

Charlie: You ought to understand that. You are the one who told me about that young rabbi who got himself nailed to a cross for doing what he felt like he had to do.

Pastor: Charlie, you push me to wonder if I ought to be going with you. I have serious doubts about what you are doing, but I am not satisfied with what I am doing either. We are in one of those situations where there is no real right answer. Let's keep praying for each other.

Charlie: Let's do. I will always love you and this church. I had better go now. (*Stands.*) Good-bye.

(*The two men embrace each other.*)

Pastor: Keep in touch.

Charlie: I will. Good-bye.

(*Charlie leaves the stage, then the pastor leaves, then the sets are removed. As the narrator begins to introduce the second act, Charlie comes in again wearing a loose fitting coat, and stands at one side of the stage.*)

Narrator: But Charlie did not keep in touch. He became more and more involved in the most extreme faction of the pro-life movement. His new church dwelt on the abortion issue almost every

Sunday. Charlie spent most of his time when he was not at work involved in pro-life activities and most of his time when he was at work thinking about it. Soon the admonitions of his old pastor were forgotten.

Then, early one morning, two months after leaving his old church, Charlie stood in the parking lot of a women's clinic with a handgun in his pocket. He was waiting for the doctor to arrive. He was surprised at how little emotion he was feeling. He was stoic in his belief that he was about to do something that had to be done.

But to Charlie's surprise, two other people arrived before the doctor.

(*Two women come onto the stage carrying pro-choice placards.*)

Deborah: Well, we are here. I wonder where the others are.

Jael: There is someone else — but he is not one of us! (*To Charlie.*) Hey, I remember you. You were one of those people demonstrating against women's freedom in front of the courthouse last month!

Charlie: You must be mistaken. I have never seen you before.

Jael: Yes, I remember you distinctly. You are part of that gang that is trying to suppress women. You are part of something evil that has been going on since the beginning of time — men always pushing women down.

Charlie: I am not trying to suppress women. I just want to stop the murder of innocent babies.

Jael: (*With rising anger.*) I believe that women ought to have the right to decide what happens to their bodies.

Deborah: Take it easy, sister.

Charlie: That wouldn't be a problem if both women and men would accept responsibility for what they do *with* their bodies.

Jael: (*Shouting*) There you go, blaming the victim. The oppressors always try to put the blame on the victims.

Deborah: Cool it, sister. Cool it.

Charlie: I don't know what you are talking about. I am not trying to oppress anyone. I am just trying to say a word for the innocent babies. It seems to me they are the victims.

Jael: You are part of what has been pushing women down and walking on them from the beginning of time.

Charlie: This is crazy. This is getting us nowhere. I am going.

Jael: You can't walk away from me like that. I won't let you. I will not be depersonalized! I will not be victimized!

(*Charlie turns and begins to walk away. Jael takes a handgun from her purse and points it at Charlie.*)

Deborah: (*Shouting*) No, Jael, don't do that!

(*Deborah grabs Jael's wrist and pushes it up so that she cannot fire. She takes the gun from Jael's hand. Jael breaks down into sobs and the two women embrace each other. Charlie stops and turns to see what has happened. He stands staring open-mouthed with amazement for a long moment, then leaves hurriedly. Deborah and Jael leave.*)

Narrator: That does raise lots of questions, doesn't it? How can we really know what is true and just and good? How can we sort out all of the ambiguities of the real issues that arise in real life? How can we sort out our own motives and feelings as we try to think through our responsibilities? Are people who try to see both sides of the big issues bound to become indecisive and ineffective in influencing the world? Is history always bound to be made only by those who allow themselves to become radicalized? And what happens to human society when it is polarized by two radicalized parties? These are questions that are hard to answer. Lots of us would like just to forget all about changing the world and concern ourselves with more comfortable things. But dare we? Here is one more question. If Christians and other people of good conscience do not undertake to shape culture and guide the course of history, who will? Someone will. But, who?

A Unison Prayer: Lord, we hear you calling us to make a difference in the world. Forgive us for wanting to hide from disturbing issues. Forgive us for trying to preserve our own comfort by closing our eyes to issues that have to do with human life and dignity. We know we should respond to your call. But we need your help. Give us the ability to see what you want for your world, even when the issues are not clear, even when partial good is the best that can be achieved, even when our own conflicting feelings confuse us. Help us to know which actions will be helpful and which will not. Show us what you want us to do, Lord, and give us the courage to do it. Amen.

---

1. Statistics available from Alan Guttenmacher Institute.

A Question Of Right And Wrong

Deuteronomy 5:1-22

Is there any such thing as right and wrong? Is there any such thing as truth? These questions bring to the surface the hidden issue behind every issue that concerns morality. Christians and others still try to make moral decisions. But we find ourselves doing that in the midst of a culture in which an increasingly large and significant part of society has decided, for better or worse, that there is no such thing as a moral decision. There is no such thing as truth, no such thing as right or wrong. It is important for us to raise again the question of whether or not there is truth and right — and we need to come to a deeper understanding than we have usually had about just what that means.

Once there was a time when there were generally held ideas about what was right and what was wrong. There were generally accepted understandings of what it meant to live a moral life. Everyone knew what was right and wrong in terms of telling the truth, respecting the property of others, observing standards of sexual morality, and not doing violence to others. There were generally accepted understandings of business ethics. Once there was a time when contracts were not necessary, there was no misrepresentation, a person's word was his bond and a handshake bound people into mutual responsibility. Once there was a philosophy of business according to which business people sought to give service as well as to make a profit. There probably never was a time when everyone did what was right, but there was a time when everyone agreed about what right is. During much of that time, most people, whether they were religious or not, would have agreed that the best statement about what is right and wrong was the Ten Commandments.

But we live in a different day today. Allan Bloom, a college professor, wrote a book that was a critical evaluation of what is going on in American Universities today. Its title is *The Closing of the American Mind.*[1] He begins with the shocking statement, "There is one thing a professor can be absolutely certain of: almost every student entering the university believes, or says he believes, that truth is relative." He says he has found that students from all sorts of backgrounds are committed to two things, relativism and equality. And he says, in the student mind, these two are related. "The relativity of truth is not a theoretical insight but a moral postulate, the condition of a free society, or so they see it." Bloom explains that students have been so convinced that every kind of conflict and abuse in human history has been caused by someone insisting that he is right and others are wrong that they have come to the conclusion that the solution to the world's problems is to do away with the ideas of right and wrong. Openness is the great virtue of our day. Allan Bloom is critical of this attitude — but he says that it is what we are up against in today's world. Have you encountered this attitude in others — or in yourself?

It is a short step from that kind of intellectual relativism to a moral relativism that believes, "I ought to be free to do anything I want to and no one has a right to be critical of anything I do. Neither do I have any business being critical of anything that anyone else does." The most conspicuous expression of this is the attitude toward sexual morality represented by most popular television programs. Many young people have been very ready to accept that attitude as their own. A large percentage of single young adults are sexually active and feel no guilt or embarrassment about it. They experience this moral relativism as a liberation from what they see as oppressive, outdated ideas — like the Ten Commandments. There is another expression of moral relativism that is less conspicuous but perhaps even more persuasive. That is relativism in business ethics. Businesses have claimed the right to do whatever will maximize profit, even if it means misrepresenting a product or the value of a property or stock, even if it means exploiting clients or employees. Persons who are involved in business are often expected to go along with these practices as a condition of their employment.

There are other expressions of moral relativism that turn up in every aspect of our lives, in education, in politics, in community life. But the expressions that we have mentioned can be taken as examples to represent a much bigger issue.

You have seen this relativism developing around you, haven't you? But have you seen it developing within you? It can sneak up on you. The attitudes that seem to be held by so many around you can suggest themselves to you when you find yourself dealing with some difficult decisions in which integrity could be costly — or with some attractive temptation. Much of our society operates on two levels today. On the theoretical level, we still profess belief in high moral standards. We still revere the Ten Commandments. But on the practical level, where the really important decisions are made, we function in terms of moral relativism. We all resent the hypocrites who talk loudly about their commitment to the Ten Commandments but cheat on their spouses and cheat us in our business dealings, if we let them. But it is easy for us to slip into it ourselves — and it is easy for us to stop expecting anything better from others.

In recent years, our country has had two bad experiences that should give us all reasons to take another look at our relativism and to make us ask if that is really how we want to organize our world and our lives.

Not too long ago, an attractive young politician ran for president. The political smut slingers exposed the fact that he had been involved in an extramarital affair. He admitted having done some things that "brought sadness to his marriage." But the country decided that didn't matter. It is significant that the country didn't actually forgive him. Instead, it decided that it didn't matter. They elected him anyway and there are many of us who believe that he did many good things while he was in office. But also while in office, he became involved in an immoral affair. It was a petty immorality when compared with some of the horrendous things that powerful people can do. But he let a little immorality intrude into a life situation that called for greatness and then tried to cover it up by being dishonest with the people. When politics finally forced him to make a public confession, it was a profound embarrassment to the whole nation and it cast a cheap shadow over many of the good things he accomplished. At the very least, that experience should make the nation ask, "Is it really true that it doesn't matter what you do in your personal life?"

The other bad experience had even more devastating effects. Bit by bit, American business drifted into the kind of "bottom line" orientation that said, "Nothing matters but making a profit." This actually became a well developed philosophy taught in university schools of business administration. That philosophy gave lots of business men the freedom to feel right about doing lots of things that everyone used to think were wrong — including misrepresenting the value of stocks and "creative" accounting practices. The collapse of the Enron and WorldCom Corporations and all the hurt that they have done have shown us what can come from that.

It is easy for us to respond in righteous indignation to things like those that compromise structures of life that everyone needs to be able to trust and respect. There will be a time for that righteous indignation. It is appropriate. But there is another question we ought to deal with first. Are we willing to put away the attractive freedom of relativism and to live up to high moral standards in our own lives? Have we found it convenient to go along with the ideas that the Ten Commandments are irrelevant and that things like adultery and dishonesty don't matter because we ourselves don't want to be held accountable for our actions? Do we like being free to do whatever is profitable without having to ask if it is right or wrong, to say whatever serves our purpose whether it is true or not, and to seek pleasure wherever we can find it without regard to basic morality? What have we learned from our country's bad experiences? What is our nation's pain and disillusionment telling us? What can we learn from the loss of integrity and of respect and of self-respect? Don't those experiences tell us that things like morality and honesty matter very much — and so do the other things that the Ten Commandments tell us?

While we are looking within, many of us can realize that we have lost something else in the relativism that says there is no such thing as truth and right and wrong. We have lost ourselves.

No, we are not talking about a "loss of innocence." Innocence is an illusion. But a person must believe some things in order to be someone. There has to be some commitment, some integrity, some character to make us significant persons or communities. Have you ever felt that you were losing that — or, perhaps, that you have lost it? We need to recover that, both as persons and as a nation.

Well, what about the question with which we began. Is there any such thing as truth? Is there any such thing as right and wrong? If there is any reality outside of our imagination, there are things that are true of it and things that are not. If there is a God, there is truth. And if it is true that God loves us and wants what is good for us, there is right and wrong.

But what about the questions that have been raised about truth? Won't convictions cause conflicts? And won't conformity to ancient rules like the Ten Commandments inhibit our ability to meet the changing demands of the future?

It is true that it is more difficult for people with differing convictions to live together in mutual respect than it is for people who are so open that they are empty. It is hard work. But people of conviction can find in each other something to respect, even if it is only the presence of conviction, and those relationships, once achieved are far richer and more significant.

And, if we understand what the Ten Commandments are all about, we will know that they are not just ancient rules that restrict our freedom and oppress us. God gave these commandments to the people of Israel as a gift of love during the time of the Exodus, the time of the liberation of Israel. They were given to make freedom and fullness of life possible, not to restrict them. God gave the commandments to the people of Israel to teach them a way that will make life hold together and work for individuals and for nations. We have discovered, or at least we should have discovered, that when they are disregarded, things start falling apart and not working.

But vital morality comes, not just from living life shaped by obedience to the commandments but from living a life shaped by a relationship with the living God who once gave the commandments. God is still out there leading us into the future just as he led the people of Israel through the wilderness. The Ten Commandments help us to know that God. So do the commandments to love God and to love our neighbor. But if we work out the shape of our lives day by day in relationship with the living God who gave those commandments, we will be able to discover what is right and true and good in each new situation of life. Furthermore, we will discover that the living God is always working to make possible what he requires so that all of the commandments become promises and give hope to the earth.

Can we hold others accountable to that standard? It would be wrong to impose our beliefs upon others. Yes, we can hope to share our faith with others, but we can't impose it upon them. And yet, there is a kind of expectation that is necessary in human community. There are certain things that people ought to be able to expect of each other. When those things are violated, damage is done to the structure of human life and of society. If we learn again to expect integrity and basic morality of each other, that expectation will tend to evoke integrity and morality. Relationship with the community can do what a relationship with God would do better.

But each of us must recover basic morality in our own lives. We must repent of our own sins. It is not enough to condemn dishonest CEOs. We must recover integrity in all of our own affairs, in family affairs, in community affairs, in political affairs, in business affairs, in *all* of our affairs, even when it is costly. It is not enough to condemn the adultery of a president. We must all repent of our own playing around with sexual immorality. When business people are away from home or when teenage couples are in cars together and when the possibility is there and the temptation is strong and when we ask, "What harm would it do?" we need to know that the answer is, "It would do a lot of harm." Immorality does damage to the very structure of human life and personhood and relatedness in persons, in families, in communities, and in nations. That is why it is wrong. People who are parts of families and communities and of nations need for the others to live up to those high moral standards that will make life hold together and work. We ought to expect that of ourselves and of each other.

Is there any such thing as truth? Is there any such thing as right and wrong? We will continue for a long time to live in a world that doubts it. But those who choose to live up to a higher standard are the hope of the world. And those who know that they live daily in relationship with the God who once gave Israel the Ten Commandments, will be those who are most able to make that work.

---

1. Allan Bloom, *The Closing of the American Mind* (New York: Simon and Schuster, 1987), ch.1.

Homosexuality, Facing The Issue

Romans 1:16-32

The Christian faith should form every aspect of the life of a Christian. For that reason, it is sometimes necessary for us to talk about things in church that we don't usually think of as religious. It is important for Christians to think through every important matter in the light of our Christian faith. Matters having to do with sexuality are like that. Most of us think of those as private matters. They are private. But they are not obscene. Our sexuality is a gift of God, a part of our humanity, given to us to bless us. But there are ways in which we can use our sexuality that cheapen it and that can be hurtful, dehumanizing, and abusive. It is important for us to understand and to live out our sexuality in reverence for God's purpose and in loving respect for ourselves and for other persons. It is important to think through the matters that have to do with sexuality in the light of the Christian faith.

One matter having to do with human sexuality has become a center of controversy in society and in the church today. It is the issue of homosexuality. Many of us are bewildered as we hear the entertainment media — which does more to shape our ways of thinking about everything than any of us want to admit — telling us that something is okay that we have always thought is wrong. And we are even more bewildered as we hear debates going on in government bodies and in the church about whether or not that is true. If our Christian faith is going to shape every aspect of our lives, we need to think that issue through in the light of our Christian faith. That is what we are going to do today. I suspect that no one — no one — is going to like where this sermon will come out because everyone on both sides of the issue wants there to be simple, clear-cut, easy answers. And the answers are not easy.

There are many of us who think that this issue is easy to understand and easy to decide about. For many, the very idea of homosexuality brings to mind something that seems totally bad and repulsive. We wonder why it has to be discussed in church. Many of us think that the people who are involved in anything like that deserve to be shut out of human society. In fact, some have let such feelings justify abusive treatment of homosexual people. But that is too easy. The issue is not that clear.

More and more of us are finding that we are acquainted with some people whom we either know to be or suspect of being homosexual and, upon reflection, we find ourselves thinking, "They seem to be nice enough people." More and more of us are having the very difficult experience of learning that someone dear to us is homosexual. That makes the matter much more difficult to deal with. If we talk with those people about their feelings, the issue becomes much more complex.

One thing is very clear. The Christian faith never gives us an excuse to despise or abuse anyone. We are called to relate to every other person in love and respect. *The Book of Discipline of the United Methodist Church*, which states the official position of that denomination on all of the difficult issues of our day, says, "... homosexual persons, no less than heterosexual persons, are individuals of sacred worth," that God's grace is available to them, that they need the ministry of the church, and that their civil rights should be respected.[1] The official teachings of many other denominations include similar statements. We can't just let our negative feelings govern us in our reaction to this issue. That is too easy — and the issue is not easy.

Many of us are also quick to say, "The Bible says that homosexuality is wrong. Certainly that ought to make the issue simple." The Bible does, in fact, make seven clear references to homosexuality and all of them either state or imply a negative judgment. The passage we have just read is probably the clearest and most definitive of those statements. We will come back around to listening to that passage before this sermon is over.

But even that does not make the issue simple or the answer easy. Christians must take seriously what the Bible says. It is the primary medium through which the living God speaks to us today. But we have learned that we sometimes have to make allowances for the influence of the cultural situation in which the biblical teachings were originally given and that we sometimes have to interpret specific teachings in the light of the total biblical witness. As a result of that, we have learned that a faithful response to the biblical teachings sometimes requires something other than a strict obedience to each requirement of the Bible writers.

The most conspicuous example of this for us probably has to do with the way in which most churches have dealt with divorce. A rigid application of biblical teachings on that subject would require that no divorced person should ever marry again. Some churches teach that. But most churches have decided that divorce is a tragic reality that breaks into the lives of many people and must be dealt with in terms of God's forgiving and healing grace. With this in mind, most have come to believe that God's compassionate response to those whose lives have been broken by divorce can allow for another marriage and another chance to put life together and make it good.

Are there some reasons to believe that the issue of homosexuality calls for some response of this kind? That is really hard to say. Most of us don't know a lot about homosexuality. What is it? Is it something that is chosen or is it something with which homosexual people are born, something they can't help? I have asked my friends in the social sciences that question and they have answered that no one knows. "The jury is still out on that issue." But they have said that they know that it is awfully hard for a homosexual person to stop being homosexual. In 1992, the General Conference of the United Methodist Church appointed a committee to study the issue of homosexuality and to make a report. They consulted the most respected scientific authorities in the country and got the same answer. It is hard for us to feel that we have all of the information we need to make informed decisions.

In our attempts to understand homosexuality, it is important to make a distinction between homosexuality as a psychological condition, and homosexuality as a lifestyle. It seems that homosexuality as a psychological condition is something over which people have varying degrees of control. It is something that needs to be dealt with in terms of God's acceptance and healing grace.

But the practice of homosexuality as a lifestyle is something about which people can make decisions. The moral teachings of the church should be understood, not as a condemnation of a psychological condition over which people may or may not have control, but as an attempt to give guidance concerning the decisions a person must make about how he or she should choose to live his or her life.

But that still does not make the matter simple. To tell a person who is of a homosexual disposition that he or she should not live a homosexual lifestyle is the same as saying that such people should live celibate lives, that they should never have the intimacy that married people are allowed to enjoy. Many people feel very bad about laying requirements on others that they themselves will not have to obey. Homosexual people say that they can't help being homosexual. Some even say that God made them that way. They feel that they, too, should be allowed to put life together in a way that meets their needs for intimate relationships.

Many people in the church feel that a compassionate response to this appeal would require the church to make some allowances for homosexual people, just as compassionate responses have been made to some others. Let me try to interpret what has been going on in the governing bodies of our denomination and others with regard to this issue. I know that lots of people can't understand what the churches are finding to argue about with regard to an issue that the Bible makes to seem so clear-cut. What is happening is not an argument for or against morality but a working through of the tensions between morality and compassion. Both morality and compassion are aspects of Christian love. Love wants what is good for the loved ones and requires what is good from them. That is morality. Love also feels with those who are loved the things that they feel, whether that is joy or sorrow or shame or pain. That is compassion. With regard to this issue, morality and compassion are in tension with each other. That is what the arguments in the church councils are all about. The issue is not an easy one to resolve. We should all be in prayer for those leaders who have to make those decisions.

Then what else should we do? Should we just agree that homosexuality is something that we can neither understand nor change, allow the homosexual people to be who they think they have to be, accept ourselves and each other as we are, and love each other? That is the recommendation of those representing homosexual people in the debates in the church. Certainly acceptance and love are essential in Christian relationships. But that makes things too easy, too. And it is not easy.

What about the matter of morality? That is a big basic question that our whole culture has swept under the rug in recent years. Traditional Christian beliefs teach us that there is a standard of right and wrong that comes from beyond us and to which we should be obedient. In our scripture lesson for today, Paul wrote out of that understanding. He believed that God created everything to work in a certain way and that God designed everything to work for the good of humankind. God taught us his way for us through his commandments but, even if a person has never heard the commandments of God, Paul believed that he or she should be able to tell what is right and what is wrong just by looking at the way God has put the world together. If people will live in reverent obedience to the will of God, life will flourish and be good for everyone. Paul, and, incidentally, Jesus too, believed that it is a part of that plan of God for the creation that "a man leaves his father and mother and clings to his wife, and they become one flesh" (Genesis 2:24).

Paul was speaking to people who lived in a Greco-Roman culture that had recreated their gods in their own image so that they could do whatever they wanted to do and feel okay about it. In that culture, sexual promiscuity, homosexuality, and even pedophilia were accepted. Paul saw the structures of human dignity and human society falling apart as a result of that. He did not say that God acted to punish those who were disobedient, just that God left them to experience the tragic results of their disobedience. He called them to seek the saving grace of God and to live in reverent obedience to God's will.

Morality is not a very popular subject in our culture today. We, too, feel that we should be free to do just whatever we find expedient or profitable or pleasurable. In fact, it is customary for us to take a very negative attitude toward anyone or anything that comes talking about our responsibility to anyone or anything beyond ourselves, especially if it makes anyone feel guilty. We take that attitude in the name of liberation and a search for fulfillment. But what has resulted is not liberation or fulfillment. The results have too often been the same kind of moral and social disintegration that Paul saw happening in the Roman world.

Our culture needs for the people called Christians to take the lead in recovering the kind of morality that seeks to know what is truly right and to live in humble obedience to it. No, it is not always easy to know what is right. But Christians ought to take seriously the teachings of the Bible, the source book of our faith, and to bow in humble reverence before it to hear what God will say to us through it about every aspect of our lives. All that we have said so far should make it clear that we do not know all that we need to know about this painful issue and that there are no easy answers. But, until we are shown a better reason to see things differently, it seems that our churches have been right in saying that, even though God loves homosexual people as much as he loves the rest of us, "... we do not condone the practice of homosexuality and consider this practice incompatible with Christian teaching...."[2] That is the teaching of The United Methodist Church and of most others.

In saying that, we have to know that we have imposed a difficult requirement upon some of our fellow human creatures. We should have a deep appreciation for the difficulty of their task. And we should take the responsibility of obedience to the moral law upon ourselves as well as imposing it upon others. We, too, must be willing to practice celibacy in singleness and fidelity in marriage. We must tell the truth whether or not it is profitable. We must stand for justice for all people even though it may sometimes seem to be to our personal disadvantage. We must all learn again to believe that the best interest of all people comes from a commitment to do justice, love kindness, and walk humbly with our God (Micah 6:8).

And it is also important to take this whole concern and set it in the context of belief in the Gospel of Jesus Christ, just as both

Paul and *The Book of Discipline of the United Methodist Church* do. Let us work through our dealing with this issue and every other issue in the knowledge that the freely-given love of God surrounds us and all other people and that God calls us to do everything in love and respect for ourselves and for all others.

---

1. "Social Principles," *The Book of Discipline of the United Methodist Church, 2000* (Nashville, Tennessee: The United Methodist Publishing House, 2000), p. 101.

2. *Ibid.*

Return From A Far Country

Luke 15:11-24

Every year, the young people in the confirmation classes are told that the most important choice they will ever make is the choice of a way of life. That choice shapes all of the others. That is true. For that reason, we should make our choice very carefully and intentionally, calling upon all of the wisdom at our command. But, all too often, the process of choosing takes place subtly and unintentionally, when we don't even know we are choosing. Today, we are going to talk about choosing a way of life.

The parable of the prodigal son, which we have just read, has many dimensions of meaning. In one of its aspects, it is a story about a young man who is choosing a way of life — and then choosing again. We can learn a lot from it.

The young man in the story grew up on a Galilean farm. There he learned a way of life that was governed by hard work, religious tradition, moral discipline — and love. He was the youngest son of the owner of the land, but he was still expected to work as hard as the hired hands. He benefitted greatly from the way of life in which he grew up — but he didn't realize it. It all seemed like drudgery to him.

This was made worse by the fact that not everyone lived in this way. His was the lifestyle of the Jewish people who were native to the land. Most Jewish people were fiercely loyal to their way of life. But their way of life had competition. Several hundred years earlier, Alexander the Great and his army marched east conquering everything in their path and trying to establish Greek culture throughout the world. At first the successors of Alexander treated the Jewish people terribly and they were regarded as the enemies. But, in time, the Roman Empire replaced the Greeks as the political power and many Jewish people began to find the Greek culture that Alexander planted attractive.

Not far from the Galilean farm where the young man lived was a region called the Decapolis. It was called that because there were ten Greek cities there, each trying to be a center of Greek culture. Theirs was a culture that emphasized material prosperity and self-indulgence. But there was much that was attractive about it. Recently, archeologists have excavated one of those cities, one called Scythopolis in the Jordan River valley. It has everything that a proper Greek city should have — and it tells a lot about the Greek way of life. It was a magnificent city with beautiful architecture adorned with columns of imported marble. There was a Grecian theater there that seated several thousand people who came to see plays dramatizing the Greek religion and world view. They had bathrooms with running water. There were arenas for competitive sports and for horse races. In the very center of the city, across the street from the town hall were the columned courts of the baths, a place where feasts were held that were orgies of self-indulgence. And next to that, an ornate circular building with lots of little rooms, the brothel. It must have all seemed very glamorous to the people who lived near there. By the time our young man came on the scene, two ways of life were competing hard for the minds and loyalties of the people.

We can just imagine that the rumors of the glamorous lifestyle of the cities of the Decapolis must have reached the hardworking young man on the Galilean farm. They must have made his work seem even more like meaningless drudgery. What would be wrong with a little self-indulgence? Finally he decided to make a break. He violated all sorts of Jewish traditions and asked his father if he could get his inheritance early, before his father died. Against his better judgment, his father gave it to him. Soon thereafter, the young man took a journey that was not long in miles but that was, in terms of a way of life, a journey to a very far country. He left the life of hard work and religious tradition and moral discipline and moved to the life of material prosperity and self-indulgence.

Do you know any other people, or peoples, who have made that change?

Our country was born out of a life of hard work and religious tradition and moral discipline. That is our heritage. We talk a lot about it and pay lip service to it. But our commitment to those values is growing thin. We admire people who work hard, but most of us don't aspire to do it. Oh, yes, we like to talk about how hard we have had to work, but that is usually part of making some claim to deserve some advantage or other which we may or may not have earned. And, while there are still many who will recommend religious tradition and moral discipline for others, it has become customary in many quarters to denigrate those things, to put them down and to equate them with hypocrisy.

There is another set of values that have won our attention. We value material prosperity and we organize our lives to get it and we celebrate it with self-indulgence. Most of us never intended for our country to exchange one set of values for another. But it has happened.

And, as individuals, many of us have participated in the change. The things that the advertisers tout in their magazine and television commercials seem so attractive. Everyone seems to be enjoying them. Why shouldn't we? We don't intend to forsake our heritage. Surely, we can still be Christians and still live what our culture calls "the good life." So we organize our lives to get affluence and once we have gotten it, we do the things that are expected of affluent people and eventually these things become the religious rituals we go through that teach and reinforce our value systems and life commitments. Since we go through those rituals more often than we go through the ones we go through in church, they battle for our souls and before we know it, we are living in Scythopolis. Now we have come to a place where many Americans cannot remember a time when life was shaped by hard work and religious tradition and moral discipline. These things sound like some grotesque ancient hypocrisy to many today.

But the young man made some harsh discoveries in Scythopolis. At first it must have seemed just as glamorous as he had expected it to be. When you have plenty of money to spend, there will be plenty of people around to help you spend it. But resources that are unreplenished soon run out. When that happened, the friends all disappeared. Everything began to fall apart. He took a job which, for a Jewish boy, must have been the most degrading one imaginable, tending unclean animals, pigs. And he got nothing to eat. And no one gave him anything.

The young man discovered what was missing from his attractive new way of life. Love was missing. I wonder if the word "love" had come to be just another word for sex in Scythopolis as it has for us. Gradually, the young man must have realized that it is really love that was behind all of that hard work and religious tradition and moral discipline that were so important in the life he lived back home. Of course, religious traditions and moral disciplines that are empty of love are indeed oppressive and hypocritical. But where everything is as it should be, religious traditions teach love and love demands moral discipline and hard work.

The young man finally got the picture. His father's hired hands were not allowed to starve as he was starving. They were given plenty to eat because his father was a man who had learned and practiced love. He decided to risk trusting his father's love and returning to his father's house. He left the place preoccupied with material affluence and self-indulgence and went back to that place of hard work and religious tradition and moral discipline — and love. He knew that what was lost was lost. But he hoped that love would make it possible for him to make a fresh start. He made his return from a far country.

You know how the story goes. Love was willing to welcome him home and to give him another chance. That is the main meaning of the parable. His father came running to meet him. Yes, it was costly for him to do that. The young man's foolishness had cost a part of the family fortune and disgraced the family in the eyes of the community. But the father was willing to absorb that cost and work with his son to help him to recover his heritage and to build another life. Certainly now he would know what hard work and religious traditions and moral discipline are all about. They are all about love.

Lots of us are making the same kinds of discoveries about the way of life so highly advertised by our popular culture. Oh, yes, that way can cause some impressive structures to grow, structures of careers and fortunes, structures of businesses and institutions and cities. But there is something missing in them, something that is needed to hold them together from the inside and to give them meaning. Without that something, impressive achievements often seem empty and flavorless and begin to fall apart.

A visitor to a great city walked in front of a building he had seen when it was new. Then, he had thought it was just about the most impressive building he knew about. It was a circular bank lobby with gleaming glass walls and bronze plaques for cornices and a cobblestone pavement outside and it was located right on Main Street. Handsome, well-dressed professional people had gone in and out to work and to trade there. But on this later visit, the visitor saw it with the windows boarded up, the bronze tarnished and the cobblestone cracked so that its artificiality could be seen. A wire gate blocked the space between it and the larger building to which it was related to keep the street people from sleeping there. But the street people were still sitting around amidst an accumulation of garbage. There was something symbolic about that. Something was missing. Things were falling apart.

Lots of us are finding businesses and families and lives falling apart because something is missing. Will we be wise enough to learn from the young man from Galilee? He made a wise decision to return from the far country. Will we make that decision, too?

Let's hope that we will not wait too long to make it. God, who is the giver of life, is always ready to welcome us back and to help us make a new start. God is willing to absorb the results of our mistakes. But worldly things deteriorate when they are neglected. In the Dallas Museum of Fine Arts, there is a painting by Thomas Hart Benton titled *The Prodigal's Return*. It shows a young man with a suit coat slung over his shoulder standing in front of a farm house. But the house is empty. Its windows are dark and the fields are overgrown from neglect, perhaps because he was not there to tend them. Let's not wait too long to return from the far country.

The choice of a way of life is the most important choice a person will ever make. It shapes everything else. We should make that choice very carefully and intentionally, calling upon all of the wisdom at our disposal. God offers us the best possibility. Behind some of the things that our culture has taught us to regard as unattractive, is a life of love. Love can hold things together. Love can make things work.

A Leper In Our Path

Matthew 8:1-4

Everyone must have been on a spiritual high as they followed Jesus down the path that day. It was probably a beautiful day. They had spent hours in a lovely place on a hillside overlooking the Sea of Galilee listening to Jesus. They had been learning about a new way of life, the way of faith and of love, a way that was very different from the rigid dogmatism of their religious traditions. Everything must have seemed right. The people must have been feeling good — like we like to feel. But then something happened that shattered their euphoria. There, in the middle of their path, was something that was both repulsive and frightening to them, a man with leprosy.

Leprosy was a terrible disease. It ate away parts of the body of an afflicted person and made them grotesque before it finally killed them. Leprosy was believed to be very contagious. Primitive laws required that anyone who had leprosy should be regarded as unclean and quarantined away from society. Anyone who touched a leper was also regarded as "unclean" until ritual purification was made. Even those who loved the lepers were required to withdraw from them. It was generally believed that there was a moral dimension to the disease, that people with leprosy were being punished by God for something bad that they had done.

No one wanted to be confronted by a leper, especially on such an occasion as the followers of Jesus were enjoying. Why did he have to be there? Why did he have to spoil the day? No doubt, many would have liked to have pretended that they had not seen the leper and gone on with their celebration. But Jesus would not have it so. The faith taught on the mountaintop had to be practiced along the path.

We are having a very similar experience today. We like to put our lives together in pleasant, prosperous ways. We like to build them out of happiness and security. We like for our religious experiences to be a part of that. We like to feel good. But there is a reality that is intruding into our experience of life that is as repulsive and as frightening to us as the leper was to those early followers of Jesus. In fact, it is remarkably similar to leprosy in many ways. It is the worldwide epidemic of AIDS. We would prefer to pretend that we do not see it. In fact, we are pushing it out of sight so that we hear and think much less about it than we once did. But it is still there, like a leper in our path, and we have to reckon with it.

By now, I am sure that you all know the basic facts about HIV/AIDS. The statistics about the worldwide epidemic are frightening. As of 2001, it was estimated that 335,359 people in the United States have the virus and 40,000 are added annually. All together, there have been 793,026 cases in the United States. 457,667 have died. Worldwide, the total number of cases has been estimated at 40 million.[1] To many of us, the statistics must seem exaggerated because we don't know of many people with the illness. But that may be because many of the people who have been infected don't yet know it and many who do know it keep their affliction secret to avoid the discrimination and hardship that could come with letting their illness be known. The victims must be all around us. We can't help being afraid. We know so little about it. What if one of our children should be infected? One young single woman confided in her pastor, "I am worried about the impact of AIDS on society — and I am worried about myself."

People respond to the epidemic in many ways. Some respond with indignation, some with fear, some with anger. All of these are understandable responses. But are they the best responses? Are they the Christian responses?

Indignation is a natural response. There is a moral dimension to the problem. Many innocent people have been infected with AIDS through blood transfusions and in other ways. Still, AIDS is being spread, in large part, by practices that most people regard as immoral, practices like both homosexual and heterosexual promiscuity and intravenous drug abuse.

Some Christians sincerely believe that AIDS is something God created to punish the homosexuals. They think it would be wrong to interfere with such a divine judgment. But that can't be right. If God worked in that way, we would all be in deep trouble for one reason or another. AIDS is simply a terrible illness and we should do all we can to cure it.

Even so, when people and societies find themselves suffering the tragic results of their own actions and lifestyles, the Bible teaches us to understand that as an experience of the judgment of God. If the AIDS epidemic is, at least in part, the result of a shallow, irresponsible, pleasure seeking lifestyle, then it certainly should call us to some form of repentance. We should be thinking about a return to morality instead of just trying to learn how to have "safe sex."

Indignation is a natural and understandable response to AIDS. But it is not the way in which Jesus responded to the leper.

Other people respond to AIDS in fear. That, too, is a natural response. It is easy for us to make idealistic statements about how we should deal with AIDS. But, when it pushes its way into your life through an encounter with someone who is infected, fear is very likely to be a dimension of the response.

A pastor recalls the feelings he had when he first went into a hospital room to call on a young man who was dying of AIDS. The pastor did not know the young man. He went because he had been asked to go by a friend. He went because he felt that it was important to make a compassionate response to a person who was dying. He knew the facts about AIDS. He knew that he was in no danger. He knew that the surgical gown and mask he wore were for the patient's protection, not the visitor's. But, when the visit was over and it was time to pray, when he reached out to take the patient's hand, the pastor found himself having to overcome some real inner resistance. He was afraid.

We can understand the panic that ensued in a certain community when people learned that a child who had been infected with AIDS by a blood transfusion had been registered in their school. We understand why there are two sides to the confidentiality issue. People who might be at risk have a right to know when a threat is present. But, if they know, will fear make them do terrible things to people who are already suffering too much? Whatever response we make to the AIDS epidemic, we will have to own and overcome our fear.

Fear is a natural response to AIDS. But Jesus did not respond to the leper in fear.

Some will undoubtedly react to the reality of AIDS with anger. We know that many people bring this disease upon themselves — and others — by choosing a lifestyle that most of us think is immoral. It is natural to be angry when someone we love does that to himself or herself, and when anyone does it to others.

One of the tragedies that has happened too often in the aftermath of the discovery of a case of AIDS in the family is that the parents have been so brokenhearted and so angry that they have rejected their son or daughter and cut themselves off from him or her. Before you condemn them for that, try to think yourself into their position. But the results compound the tragedy. The infected person is forced to endure the slow and painful process of dying alone, without financial support, and — worse — without the loving relationships of the family. And the family must suffer terribly during that process, too. It is useless to say, "Don't be angry." Anger just happens. It will have to be dealt with when it is there.

Anger and rejection are natural reactions to AIDS. But Jesus did not respond to the leper in anger or in rejection.

Christ calls us to move beyond all of these natural reactions and to respond in a very different way to the reality of AIDS and to those who are its victims. When Jesus turned aside on that day to make a compassionate response to the leper who was in his path, he demonstrated another way of responding to human suffering. Those who would be followers of Jesus must learn how to respond in loving compassion.

Love will require us to seek a cure for AIDS and to call for a renewal of morality and to do all sorts of practical things to limit the spread of the epidemic.

Love should make Christian people teach and model a way of life that will cause the epidemic not to spread. A significant story comes out of Southeast Asia, where the AIDS epidemic has reached terrible proportions. Among the mountain villages of Thailand, there is one village where virtually 100 percent of the population is infected with AIDS. But in the next village, there is not a single case. What made the difference? Many years ago, a Lutheran missionary came to the second village and the people all accepted the Christian faith. Since that time, the people of that village learned and lived a lifestyle that does not include sexual promiscuity. It seems that the world could learn something from that village.

But love must also make a personal response to those who suffer. We can understand that. A few years ago, a church women's group undertook to make thousands of warm receiving blankets for little babies who were being born infected with AIDS. It is a natural thing to want to make a loving response to the suffering innocent.

But what about those who are not innocent? Can there be any warm blanket of love for them? Some people will say, "No, we must respond to wrong behavior in a way that will condemn it! A loving response might encourage it!" But we did not learn that response from Christ. No one ever had higher moral expectations than did Jesus. Yet, when people suffered — even because of their moral failures — Jesus was there to love, to help, and if possible to heal. We should know that. We are all beneficiaries of the compassionate response of Christ. Can any of us claim to have deserved God's love?

Can we respond in that way to others, even others with AIDS?

Listen to a story. It is a true story. There was a certain church that had a pastor whom everyone loved and admired. For years, he had been there for them. He had loved them and cared for them and preached the Christian faith to them by word and by example. He had lived among them and raised his children among them and made the whole life of their community better through his ministry.

Then one day one of the pastor's adult sons came back home to live with his parents. He was ill. His parents were caring for him. Eventually, the word went through the community that the pastor's son had AIDS.

How would the church react? This was a down-to-earth, middle American community with old-fashioned moral values. They might have been expected to get angry at the pastor and reject him, saying that he must not have practiced what he preached since he had failed as a parent. They might have been expected to get angry at the son for letting the pastor and the church down. They might have been expected to withdraw from the whole family in natural fear. Any of these things might have happened. But none of them did.

Instead, the church gathered around the pastor and his family and his afflicted son. They surrounded them with loving compassion. They visited. They helped with nursing duties. They washed the linens. They did all they could to help the family through the time of tragic suffering. And when death came, the whole community mourned. That sort of thing can happen. We know that it can happen — because it did.

In recent years, more and more churches are learning to make a compassionate response to people with AIDS. Working out of a center in Houston, Texas, two ministers, Ron Sunderland and Earl Shelp, have helped churches across the country organize care teams to offer a ministry of "sustaining presence" to people with AIDS. In fourteen years, they have seen 3,800 people become involved in care team ministries and these have ministered to 1,850 people with AIDS.[2]

In Jesus's day, religious laws forbade anyone to touch a leper. But Jesus reached out and touched the leper because loving compassion required him to. In our day, all sorts of things within us and around us forbid us to get involved with people who have AIDS — or even with the issue itself. But if we are followers of Jesus, we will. We will reach out in love — and touch. That may not make the disease go away. But there are other ways in which a loving touch can heal.[3]

---

1. Statistics from the Center For Disease Control.

2. Earl E. Shelp and Ronald H. Sunderland, *Sustaining Presence: A Model For Caring By People of Faith* (Nashville: Abingdon Press, 2000).

3. A version of this sermon was originally published in *Preaching*, January-February 1999, Michael Duduit, Editor (Franklin, Tennessee: Preaching Resources, Inc.).

War Against Hate

1 John 3:11-24

A short time ago, the evening news on television reported that a man had gone on a shooting binge. He had gone into a Jewish child care center and shot several people, including some little children. Then he killed a Filipino American postman. He said that he intended to signal to the American people that it is time for everyone to rise up and kill Jews. He said he was acting on behalf of a white supremacist group called "Christian Identity."

At first, that looks to most of us like a freak occurrence that hardly deserved the attention of a sermon. Everyone knows that hate crimes are repulsive. And everyone knows that the only way in which you can call a hateful action against another person "Christian" is to forget about Jesus of Nazareth and all that he did and all that he said. We all know that.

And yet, that same kind of hateful action keeps happening again and again at every level of human life and human society and sometimes it explodes into monstrous tragedies that dominate human history. We remember a time when that kind of thinking took possession of one of the most advanced and supposedly Christian nations of the world with the results that six million Jews were killed, the world was plunged into the most inclusive war it had ever known, and destructive conflicts were spun off that are still active currents in human history today. When that war was over, we thought nothing like that would ever happen again — but it has. During the partitioning of India, in Cambodia, in Nigeria, in Northern Ireland, in the Middle East, in El Salvador and other parts of Central and South America, in Burundi and Rwanda, and most recently in Bosnia and Kosivo and in Israel, populations have been split into warring hate groups and terrible atrocities have been committed. It is hard for us to imagine the amount of human death and hurt these things have caused. Most of us don't try to imagine it because we really couldn't handle it. But it is real. And similar things can happen at lower levels of human life and history, within persons, within families, within communities. This demands our attention. If we do not do something about it, it can destroy us all — and we know that.

The whole history of humanity is a story of a cosmic war between love and hate. Love is that force that is committed to pulling things together and building things up and making life truly good for everyone. Hate is that force that pulls things apart. It sets people and groups and races and nations against each other in destructive conflict. The battle goes on within each individual person, and within groups like the student bodies of high schools, or within communities. We have made a lot of progress in the relationship between races in our country but we are not yet beyond the danger of destructive conflicts between races. And it goes on within nations and between nations.

It should be clear now that we have addressed a topic that is much too big to be dealt with in just one sermon. But we have to say something. We have to remind ourselves that the faith we profess requires us to be participants in that awful conflict as agents of love. The passage from 1 John makes that clear. So does the whole New Testament. Jesus came to show us God's love, to teach us how to love, to love us into loving, and to send us out into the world as agents of love. That is what it is all about.

At first this idea of a conflict between love and hate seems farfetched because most of us live most of the time neither loving nor hating but in a kind of benign selfish indifference that we call minding our own business. But indifference usually does nothing to oppose hate and it can easily be stampeded into participating in hatred. Only those who love can effectively oppose hate. And love is a rare thing. It is hard to come to, costly to practice, and difficult to sustain in the midst of conflict.

Let's talk some about the dynamics of indifference and hate and love.

Indifference is basically a selfish way of life. We go happily along thinking of ourselves, pursuing our own dreams, and evaluating everyone and everything in terms of how it affects our personal interest. Indifference can sometimes hurt others by doing thoughtless little things that have a greater impact than may have been intended. Snobbishness or ridicule can happen. Some of the young people who have recently committed crimes in their schools explained that they had been made to feel like outsiders by their classmates. Racial epithets are often easy to toss out. But their impact can hurt terribly when they land in the life of someone who is already sore from discrimination and abuse. By contrast, a person who is "minding his or her own business" can be angered by someone who interferes with that business or threatens his or her well-being.

Hate, too, begins with self-interest. It can begin as a reaction to an injustice or an injury, either real or perceived. When there is an injustice or an injury, anger is an appropriate response. Anger focuses upon the issue or the event and tries to do something to make it right. But when the anger turns into lingering bitterness and focuses upon the people or groups that we perceive as the offenders, then hate can grow. Fear can generate hate, too. In fact, hate is sometimes just fear acting brave. Hate usually happens when we depersonalize another person or group. We stop thinking of them as people like ourselves, people who have fears and hopes and needs, and start thinking of them just as things, things for which we make up derogatory names, things that we will come to think of as our enemy.

Try to understand, hate is not a freakish thing. It is an attempt by some person who feels vulnerable to hold on to identity and well-being. Sometimes it is hard not to hate. There are some situations in life that are hard to live through without hating, situations like war or oppression or discrimination or poverty.

But hate has a way of multiplying itself. Hate wants to strike out against the one who is perceived as the enemy to get revenge for injuries or to defend self against threats. Once the blow is struck, the one who is struck feels compelled to strike back. The conflict can spread and escalate in terrible ways. Those who are most committed to hateful purposes have learned how to manage the escalation of hostilities to serve their purpose and to force confrontations. We have seen this happening on both sides in the conflict between Jews and Palestinians in the Middle East. We have seen it happen in other places, too.

Of course, those who hate usually give their hate another name, like nationalism (that is the one Hitler used) or ethnic pride. Real nationalism and real ethnic pride are good things. But when the reality the words represent is really hate, a destructive force can grow and feel noble about doing bad things.

Now and again, groups that identify themselves by their religion may be caught up in the tragic eddies of hatred. This is especially bad when a group has learned to identify itself by its religion but has forgotten what its religion teaches. Then a person may do hateful things in the name of religion and feel that he or she is doing them in the service of God. History from ancient times to the present has been full of tragic examples of this. The American people were all shocked by the revelation that hatred of America is being taught to young boys in religious schools in many parts of the Arab world. How, we wonder, can people make hate into a religious virtue? But the same thing has happened in certain Christian communities. In her book, *The Battle For God*, Karen Armstrong traces the development of Jewish, Christian, and Muslim religion in the history of the modern era. She makes reference to a "theology of hate" that emerges from time to time in all three religions.[1]

A story is told of a certain Muslim woman who got trapped in the terrible conflicts of what once was Yugoslavia. She was a teacher and she said she had always taught that people should love each other. But in the course of the struggle, her neighbor's teenage son dragged her out into the street one day where they were surrounded by a jeering crowd of his friends and there he did something so degrading and disgusting to her that it won't do to describe it here. As he did it, he jeered, "That is all you are good for, you filthy Muslim woman!" So terrible was the experience that the woman named her next child "Jihad" and said to him as he nursed each day, "May you strangle on my milk if you ever forget what was done to me." The young man who did this was a Christian. He probably thought that he was acting in defense of his Orthodox Christian faith, even though the leaders of his church were crying out against the conflict.[2] Sometimes it is hard not to hate.

Hate is a terrible and destructive thing. It can fester and grow and spread. It destroys the humanity of both the hater and the hated. It can result in a depressed student shooting at his classmates — or in one nation firing nuclear weapons at another. It can destroy us all. The writer of 1 John calls things what they are. Hate leads to the murder of our brothers and sisters. And indifference to our neighbor's needs is one step on the way to hate.

Only love can effectively oppose and overcome hate. It must be clear that the love we are talking about now is more than just a warm emotion. It is the kind of commitment to life that we see at work in God. 1 John tells us something of the dynamics of love. Love comes to us as a gift from God. But it must be chosen. We must choose to know ourselves as people who are loved by God. That is awfully important. Many whom God loves choose not to let that love into their lives. It is knowing that we are loved that sets us free from the fears that make many people hate. And we must also choose to be people who love. There are lots of other ways to live a life. It takes a real commitment to live your life in love.

Love makes us live in some unique ways. For instance, love does not treat other people as if they were just things. Love always treats people like persons, persons like ourselves. Love teaches us to care about others — all others. Love is always reaching out to make life better and to build people and communities up. These things come naturally for one who loves.

But loving can be costly and difficult in a situation in which love is in conflict with hate. 1 John says, "Don't be astonished, brothers and sisters, when the world hates us." It comes with the territory. It can be costly to reach out and try to be responsive to human need in our world, especially since there is so much of it. And it can be costly to speak out against hate, especially when people are practicing it in the name of nationalism or ethnic pride or their religion. In those cases, acting in love may cause some to do bad things to you. Then you will be tempted to give in to an answering hate and to return hurt for hurt. If you do that, you lose and hate wins and we are all in jeopardy. We have to learn the strategy of returning good for evil and of overcoming evil with good. That is how love works. Remember, the real enemy is not the person or the group that seems to be opposing you. The real enemy is hate. The objective is to get both them and yourself free of hate.

There may be times when hate will become so militant that loving people will have to try to contain it militarily. But we must always remember that winning the military victory does not solve the problem. In fact, having to make a military or forceful response only makes matters worse. The real solution must be accomplished through the difficult strategies of forgiving and being reconciled and building up.

I know that all of this sounds very idealistic. If you have experienced the real struggle with hatred in the real world, you are wanting to cry out, "It is not that easy, preacher!" In the harsh situations of real life, these things are hard to do. But they are possible. And they offer our only hope. In South Africa, the people all knew that they were going to have to forgive each other and to work together to build a new order. But before forgiving could happen, they knew that the atrocities of the past would have to be faced and acknowledged. To forgive without a recognition of evil done and an acceptance of responsibility would be to dishonor the suffering of all who had suffered injustice. So they appointed a "Truth Commission" to hear the confessions of those who are to be pardoned. We have to reckon with the enormity of the damage done by hate. We have to reckon with the hate that has sometimes grown in ourselves. But we must somehow overcome hate if humanity is to survive.

The battle against hate must be carried out on every level of human life. And we have to begin by overcoming the hate that may be growing in our own lives. We will not be able to succeed if we do not stay in touch with God whose love enables our own. We must abide in him and obey his commandments.

1 John said, "We know love by this, that Jesus laid down his life for us. We also ought to lay down our lives for one another." There is a war going on between love and hate in our lives, in our communities and in our world. God is waging the war against hate,

and all who are called Christian are called to participate in his loving work.

---

1. Karen Armstrong, *The Battle for God* (New York: Ballantine Books, 2000), p. 84 and others.

2. Miroslav Volf, *Exclusion and Embrace* (Nashville: Abingdon, 1996), p. 111.

Breaking Down Walls

Ephesians 2:11-22

Through Christ, God has solved the problem of conflict between races.

The description of God's saving work that we find in the Bible is much broader and more comprehensive than the description we find in today's popular piety. Yes, it does have to do with God saving us from guilt and death so that we can live with God eternally after we die. But it also has to do with God saving us from those things that keep us from living lives that are full and good and loving here and now. And, it has to do with God saving human society as a whole from those things that are hurtful and destructive and contrary to God's loving purpose for us.

Racial conflict is one of the things from which we need to be saved. That was as true in the days in which the letter to the Ephesians was written as it is today. Jews and Gentiles, that is the non-Jews of the Greco-Roman society, had no use for each other. They had grievances against one another and hostilities toward each other. These animosities were probably made worse by their recent history. This letter was probably written near the time when Jewish nationalists rebelled for the last time against the Roman empire and were defeated by the Roman legions. The Romans marched into Jerusalem and destroyed the Temple which was the center of Jewish life and worship. After that, a small band of Jewish Zealots took refuge in the mountaintop fortress of Masada in the Judean wilderness. They were besieged by the Roman army until, when the fortress seemed destined to fall, the Jews committed mass suicide rather than be captured by their hated enemy. The bitterness that had grown up between the two groups must have been terrible.

But the writer of the book of Ephesians says, "For he [Christ] is our peace; in his flesh he has made both groups into one and has broken down the dividing wall, that is, the hostility between us.

He has abolished the law with its commandments and ordinances, that he might create in himself one new humanity in place of the two, thus making peace, and might reconcile both groups to God in one body through the cross, thus putting to death that hostility through it" (Ephesians 2:14-16). Christ has broken down the wall. As a part of God's saving work, Christ has put an end to hostility between races.

When we hear that, most of us feel compelled to say, "Hey, wait a minute! Something must have gone wrong. Christ is supposed to have put an end to hostility but we can clearly see that the hostility and the dividing walls are still very much with us." If this saving work has been accomplished by God through Christ, then it must be, like so many other saving works, something that our world has yet to appropriate. It must be another of those gifts of God that we still need to grow into.

Racial conflicts are still very much with us. Our newspapers keep bringing us reports of violent conflicts between ethnic groups on every continent on earth. And in America, the structure of racial conflict has grown even more complex. It has to do, not only with conflicts between Black and White Americans, but also between Hispanic Americans and Asian Americans and Native Americans and Arab Americans and other groups with the rest of American society. The conflict that usually comes to mind first, because it has received so much attention in recent years, is the conflict between African Americans and others in American society.

With regard to that conflict, many of us have a reaction similar to the reaction we have to the idea that God has put an end to racial conflict through Christ. We think, "That conflict was supposed to have been over by now." But it isn't.

Many of us remember the Civil Rights movement of the '60s. We remember Martin Luther King, Jr., sharing his dream of an America in which Black and White people would live together in mutual respect and justice. That movement brought about significant changes in the legal and institutional structures of our country. Schools were integrated. Discrimination on the basis of race was made illegal. Changes took place in the social structures of our land. Most of our churches did away with the formal structures of segregation and began to work intentionally at rooting out residual discrimination.

Some of us remember the trauma of that time of change. Some of us remember how costly it could be to participate in a demonstration. Some of us remember the great convulsions of anger and hatred that took place in response to those demonstrations. Some of us remember how it felt from one side and some of us remember how it felt from the other side. Some of us remember the riots that erupted in some places when well-ordered, intentional actions got lost in a turmoil of frustration and fear. Many pastors can remember how frightening and how lonely it could be to speak out in favor of racial brotherhood during those days. But all of that is behind us now and everything is supposed to be different.

Some things are different. There are no more lynchings. There are no more "White Only" restrooms or water fountains or restaurants. Now people no longer make loud racist speeches in all kinds of social settings and claim — and feel — that they are speaking for the majority. Public opinion has shifted in favor of racial justice — at least in the abstract form. Some things are different.

But some things that we thought would be different are not. Some of us thought that, by now, there would be no more White and Black churches, and that young people in public schools would have forgotten who is White and who is Black, and that we would no longer have to rely on quotas to ensure equitable employment opportunities, and that everyone could count on equal treatment by law enforcement officials. Not all of those things have happened. Some have felt that there is a need to retain Black churches and social groups to preserve the values of Black culture and to give support to people who feel vulnerable in a society they have not yet learned to trust. There may be good reasons for making some modifications to Dr. King's dream. But that is not the real problem. The real problem is that the dividing walls are still there. They may not be there in terms of physical or legal or social structures, but they are there in other forms — and the hostility is still there, too.

The hostility is there on both sides of the racial lines. White people and Black people have hurt each other and they can't forget it. Everyone knows the terrible ways in which White people have hurt Black people in the history of this country. The injuries and the injustices have been massive. But there is also a history of the ways in which Black people have hurt White people. It is much less massive — but to those who have experienced it, it is real. There is nothing to be gained by reciting a catalogue of inflammatory grievances. But if I were to tell you the things that White people have told me they have suffered from Black people, I believe that people of both races would have to say, "Yes, that was wrong." The hurts have accumulated on both sides and so have the frustrations and the bitterness — and the hostility. The fact that we don't talk about it only makes it worse. The hostility is there in both groups. And any proposal for solving our racial problems that suggests that one group or the other will have to do all of the changing will not serve our needs. We all share this problem. We will all have to work together to solve it.

There is a neighborhood that has integrated. We once thought that would be the solution to all of our country's problems. This neighborhood of pleasant small homes was built right after the Second World War. Young White families moved in because they believed it would be a happy place to live and a good place to raise their children. They thought they would never want to live anywhere else. Community life was active and good. Then, when things began to change in our country, Black families began to move in. They, too, wanted to live in a nice neighborhood where community life would be good and they could find a good place to raise their children. The Whites did not immediately leave. Many stayed. Both groups hoped that the neighborhood would still be a good place to live. But it hasn't worked out that way.

Some friendships were formed across racial lines. But it was not easy for the Black people to forget their bitter past. They had experienced racial insults and discrimination — and those things have not stopped. They do not believe that they have equal opportunities — and they are sorely tempted to explain all of their failures and frustrations by blaming them on discrimination. They do not believe that they receive equal treatment from law enforcement people. When one of their own gets into trouble with the law, they tend to rally to the support of that person rather than asking if the person was indeed guilty of breaking the law. A grievance may trigger a potentially volatile reaction. There is much disappointment and frustration and hostility. They do not find their neighborhood a happy place to live.

And the White people who remained, who thought they would never want to live anywhere else, live in fear. They put burglar bars on the doors and windows of their houses and they don't go out after dark. One elderly man who is crippled, sits day after day facing the door of his little house with a loaded shotgun within reach because he fully believes that he will one day have to use it to protect himself and his wife against one of his neighbors who will come to do them harm.

Yes, there are a few who have formed interracial friendships. Yes, there are some who are working to build a better community. But, for the most part, the quality of relationships in the community is one of fear and hostility — on both sides. The dividing walls are there. And here is the worst part. No one is talking about it. As the prophet Jeremiah once said, "They have treated the wounds of my people carelessly saying, 'Peace, peace' when there is no peace" (Jeremiah 6:14). Because no one will talk about the problems, no one sees any hope that they will get better. The frustrations increase — and with them the hostilities — and with that, the possibility that some violence will eventually erupt that will devastate all of their lives.

That community is probably not a unique one.

What happened to that saving work of God through which the dividing walls of hostility were supposed to have been broken down? If that is a salvation that still has to be appropriated, how can we do that?

How did it happen in the community to which the letter to the Ephesians was first written? It started by leading people into a new understanding of who they were and how they were related to reality as a whole. It was an understanding that did not depend either upon the Jewish religious laws or upon the Greco-Roman cultural heritage that they had once counted on to make their lives work. It depended rather upon the belief that they were the beloved children of the eternal God who created all things. When they found their ways into that relationship, they were set free to let go of the things they once depended upon — the things that made them anxious about anyone who did not share those things and that set them against all who were different. When Jewish Christians and Gentile Christians found that they had the most important thing in their lives in common, a community grew up that included them all. The walls were broken down. To be sure, they were still just a small community of reconciled people in a larger community that was still divided by hostilities. But they were an example that showed the world a new possibility. And we can imagine that, as they went about trying to reconcile others with God, they also tried to help them make peace with one another.

Where can we start if we want to appropriate that kind of salvation? We have to start by taking our Christian understanding of who we are into the center of our being and by letting that shape our lives instead of all of the other things that have been shaping us. We have to let go of all of the bitterness and anger and fear — or all of the pretensions either of righteousness or of superiority — that we have allowed to tell us who we are. Instead, we must insist on simply knowing ourselves as children of God and on living out of that self-understanding. Until we can do that, we will not be free to move ahead.

But what do we do next? The biblical model seems to depend upon the person on the other side of the wall making the same discovery. We cannot do that for another. But we can attribute to the other — and to all others — the same status of children of God that we have claimed for ourselves. That will enable us to approach others with a kind of respect that they may not understand at first. Maybe they will eventually learn to understand it, and to trust it, and maybe even to choose it for themselves.

Then we have to take the courageous and audacious step of talking with each other. No, it is not enough just to make polite conversation and to say the little right things that we know we are supposed to say in interracial dialogues. We have to dare to share with the others the things we have experienced and to tell them how we have felt about it. Then we have to invite the others to tell us how they feel and listen deeply and appreciatively to them. It will not be easy. We may have to find our ways into conversation slowly and laboriously. And it may not be a pleasant experience. But it will be constructive. It will be a start toward breaking down the walls.

There is a church in another city that was built out of the merger of two older congregations, one White and one Black. The pastor who led the church through its merger said that the most important thing they did was to get the members of the two churches together and let them talk and talk and talk. Now the merged congregation carries on a vital congregational life that is a witness to the possibility that dividing walls of hostility can be broken down.

We should start having these conversations in our churches. There is already supposed to be some community there. Maybe there will still be White churches and Black churches but we can intentionally get together to talk about the things that are important to us. Churches used to go through the motions of doing that now and then. We need to do it some more — and do it better. Then, as opportunities present themselves — or, as we are able to create opportunities — we need to talk with others outside of the church, person to person, group to group, about the things that are tearing us up inside and threatening to tear up our world if we don't do something about them. Just talk for starters. But really talk. We may be surprised where that will take us.

We may be surprised to find that the risen Christ can again work through our interactions to break down the walls of hostility, and to make us one, and to give us peace.

Landsberg

John 12:27-33

On Memorial Day we remember the sacrificial service of people who have fought and died in our country's wars. Recently, the movie *Saving Private Ryan* has reminded us of the horror of the Second World War and Tom Brokaw's book *The Greatest Generation* has reminded us of the courage of the people who fought it. Our world needs to be reminded of the profound lesson that some learned from that experience. It was a lesson about the utter futility of war and of the urgency of the world's need to learn a better way for peoples and nations to live together in this one small world we inhabit. Let me tell you a story that may help you to remember. It is a story about something that actually happened.

One beautiful afternoon in the summer of 1990, a tour bus full of American church people traveled across the beautiful German countryside on the way to Oberammergau. They were going to see the famous passion play. The pastor, who was leading the group, sat looking out the window and enjoying the scenery. It was Sunday afternoon and he had asked the guide to find a place to hold a vesper service. He had prepared a talk and he reviewed the message in his mind as he gazed out the window. The country was beautiful. The people seemed prosperous and happy. German young people were racing around the countryside on expensive motorcycles. They would later see others paragliding off of the mountaintops. Everything was beautiful. But the pastor could not stop remembering that this was the country with which his country had been at war once while he was young. The memories of the stories that had come back from that war were not beautiful.

Evidently, another member of the group was having similar thoughts. An older man, who had fought his way across this part of Germany as a combat infantryman, came and sat in the seat across the aisle from the pastor and started fumbling with a map and looking out the windshield for landmarks. He said, "There is supposed to be a town called Landsberg up here somewhere. We liberated a German concentration camp there." He told of the half-starved Jewish prisoners, of the wagons full of corpses, of the long trenches prepared for their burial. He said, "It was there that I finally understood why I needed to leave my home and go to war." Landsberg had another distinction. A young Adolf Hitler was put in prison there for his early political activities. While he was there he wrote, *Mein Kamph*. The old soldier saw no familiar landmarks so he folded his map and went back to his seat wondering if Landsberg still exists.

The pastor's mind wandered back to a trip he had taken the previous year to Coventry England. There he had visited the cathedral which had been destroyed by German firebombs. On the day after the bombing, a priest wandered across the nave of the burned-out shell of the building. He found it littered with great, old handmade nails from the burned roof. He picked up three of them and fastened them together into a unique cross that has now become a familiar symbol. He stood it on what was left of the altar in the hope that the cathedral would rise again. It did, indeed, rise again. The ruins of the old church were left as a reminder of the destructiveness of war. But, with the help of people all over the world, a new cathedral was built. It became a center of Christian ministries of reconciliation and peace. People from all over the world became involved in those ministries. And the symbol of those ministries was the Coventry cross of nails.

The guide interrupted the pastor's thoughts by telling him that they were coming to a place where there might be a church in which they could hold a vesper service. The pastor had explained to the guide that they really didn't need a church building, but she didn't seem to understand that. The town looked like an attractive modern suburb of some city. Soon the bus was parked in front of a church. The guide found that the building was locked but that there was a courtyard in which the group could hold a worship service. The building caught the pastor's attention immediately. There was something very special about this building. It was a stucco building with a steeple through which worshipers entered a courtyard.

On top of the steeple was a Coventry cross. The pastor was amazed to see that symbol there in Germany. It soon became apparent that there was even more to ponder. The building was an architectural sermon. It preached the same sermon that the Coventry cathedral preaches. As the group entered the courtyard through the base of the steeple, they found themselves surrounded by heavy wooden plaques, written in different languages: German, English, French, Spanish, Italian, Greek, yes, and Hebrew. Each one saying "Be reconciled to God," as if there is no other reason why anyone should enter that place. And over their heads hung a heavy metal sculpture representing a crown of thorns, suggesting that the only way to be reconciled to God is through the suffering of Christ. In the courtyard was a fountain on the bottom of which was a mosaic representing the sign of Jonah. The pastor remembered that, just after the Second World War, there was a play that was presented all over Germany. It dramatized the need for repentance among the German people. It's title was *The Sign of Jonah*.

The pastor wandered around taking in all of the things that surrounded him and rapidly replacing the sermon he had prepared with one he was preparing on the spot. About that time, a young woman appeared. She had come to practice on the organ and she invited the group to come into the sanctuary for their vesper service. In the sanctuary, another Coventry cross stood on the altar and behind it hung a tapestry depicting Jesus on the cross, reaching out to those around him. There were stylized representations of human hands of all colors reaching out to him. Under it was an inscription in German, "I, when I am lifted up from the earth, will draw all people to myself" (John 12:32).

For the vesper talk, the pastor simply interpreted the message of the building. He reminded the group that a great wave of repentance and spiritual renewal had swept the German nation right after the Second World War. That repentance had prepared the way for the resurrection of the nation. The building was a witness that, in Germany as well as in other countries, those who had fought most bravely and suffered most deeply had come away with a conviction of the utter futility of war, and a commitment to find a better way for the world, a way of reconciliation pioneered by the suffering Christ who came to show us how to love each other.

Some of you may remember that, right after the Second World War, there were many serious efforts to find a way to enable the peoples of the world to live together in peace. The United Nations was formed. Many people became missionaries, hoping to teach the world to love. A former chaplain, who could never forget holding a young soldier in his arms while he bled to death, organized World Vision, an interfaith organization dedicated to wiping out hunger and doing a work of reconciliation among people. Many took seriously the possibility that Jesus really had shown us the way that is the hope of the world, a way of reconciliation and love.

But somehow, in the years that followed, the noble vision got lost. There was the cold war. Fear grew and turned to hatred. People again began to think that the only safety is to be found in preparing for and waging war. You hardly ever hear anyone talking about reconciliation any more. If someone does suggest that there may be nonviolent ways of building a better world, most people respond by saying, "That would be nice, but it just isn't practical."

Recently, a theologian by the name of Walter Wink wrote a book in which he challenged that assumption. He listed the times in recent history when nonviolent ways of achieving social change were given a chance. He mentioned Gandhi's movement for the liberation of India. He mentioned the American Civil Rights movement. He mentioned the Solidarity movement in Poland and the movements that finally resulted in the dismantling of the Berlin Wall. All of those efforts have accomplished lasting and significant social change.[1] But the history of warfare has shown that war always generates hostilities that fester until they break out into more wars. It may sometimes be necessary for nations to go to war. But when the war is over, the real problems still have to be solved, under more difficult conditions, in other ways.

Jesus came teaching a way of love. The world has never really caught the vision of what that could mean. We have never really sought to know what it would mean for nations to learn the way of reconciliation and respect. There are still some who believe that there is a real and practical and effective way to make love the strategy for solving the problems and resolving the conflicts of the world. The world probably came as close as it has ever come to catching that vision in the aftermath of the Second World War. But then the vision faded away and an obsession with warfare replaced it.

Now our country still spends much more on military preparedness than is needed to maintain an adequate defense. Congress often appropriates more than the Pentagon asks for. And when there is a problem we can't solve in the world, we send in the bombers. Shouldn't we be trying to learn a better way, a way that can actually produce peace with justice?

As the tour group walked back to the bus after the vesper service on the way to Oberammergau, the German driver came up to the pastor and said he had just discovered that the borrowed church was actually the chapel of a German army base. The pastor was amazed. He asked the driver the name of the town. He fumbled with his maps, studied the location, and said, "Landsberg." The pastor felt a chill of excitement sweep over his body. The fact that the chapel of the German army base in Landsberg was built to preach a sermon about reconciliation means that someone had once caught a vision.

There were those who learned the lesson that terrible war taught, but too few. And the way of love and reconciliation was evidently too hard to learn, and the way of war had evidently been learned too well. It seems we have forgotten that when we allow fear to rule, we can be turned into tyrants, and that when we resort to war to solve the world's problems, only war wins. But if Jesus Christ were lifted up, would he be able to draw all peoples to him? There was a folk song that came out of another time in history when the world's heart was being broken by war. It asks the question, "When will we ever learn? When will we ever learn?"

---

1. Walter Wink, *Engaging the Powers* (Minneapolis: Fortress, 1992), pp. 244-251.

Message From Medjugorje

John 15:12-17

A number of years ago, a certain young man was going from church to church telling about an experience he had on a pilgrimage to an obscure little place in central Europe called Medjugorje. It seemed that he was part of the Roman Catholic charismatic movement. He had obviously been deeply moved by what he had experienced and was eager to share it.

A few years before that time, in June of 1981, some teenagers had been walking in the hills near the village of Medjugorje where they lived and they had a very special experience. They reported that the Virgin Mary had appeared to them and had given them messages from her son, Jesus. The first encounter came to two young girls. When the first one saw what she thought was the Virgin Mary, she said, "Look, it's Our Lady." The other girl said something like, "Oh, come on now, why would Our Lady appear to us?" But the next day, they returned with a few of their friends and the Virgin appeared to them again and spoke to them and promised to keep meeting them and giving them messages from Jesus. In fact, the young people reported that Mary continued to appear to them and to give them messages to convey to others. The content of the messages has been varied. Much of it has to do with the practices of Christian piety that are parts of the Roman Catholic tradition. It seems that the summary of the messages could be contained in two appeals. The first is, "Return to your faith." The second appeal is, "Love one another." Mary said Jesus wants the people to learn to live together in love, not just with their Roman Catholic neighbors, but with everybody. The appearances continued to occur for several years.

The news of the appearances soon spread throughout the world. People began to come from the distant parts of the earth to be in the presence of something miraculous. In fact, many miraculous healings were reported. Many people, like the young man who spoke, went home with hearts full of inspiration.

Now most of us will have to admit that we really don't quite know what to make of the report. Most of us are neither Roman Catholic nor charismatic and the whole thing seemed quite foreign to us. (The truth is that many in the leadership of the Roman Catholic Church are still scratching their heads about it.) But as strange as the whole thing seemed, one thing rings true. The message. If Jesus actually were going to send a message to this world we live in, it might very well be just what the young people reported, "Return to your faith," and "Learn to live together in love." Paul told us to test any spirits that claim to have messages from God by asking whether or not they confess that Jesus Christ is Lord (1 Corinthians 12:3). We can take that to mean, "Ask whether or not the message corresponds to what Jesus taught us because Jesus is the Lord." This message passes the test.

That leaves us with just one question. "Why would God do something this extraordinary to deliver a message that anyone who has the least acquaintance with the Christian faith would already know?" God doesn't usually use miracles like that. This question is the same as the one raised by the young girl on the hill the first time the Virgin Mary was said to have appeared to them. "Come on now. Why would the Virgin Mary appear to a couple of kids who were out for a walk?" What is the urgency of the occasion? Many who heard the young man's report wondered about that for a long time.

But eventually we got an answer to our question. You see, the little town of Medjugorje is located in Bosnia. At that time, it was a country in which there were deep hatreds that had existed between religious and ethnic groups for centuries. The people had been forced to live together in peace by the rule of a tyrant — and most of the people had learned to get along together as neighbors — but the tyrant's days were numbered. There was a great danger that the old hatreds could assert themselves and tear the country into parts and set the parts against each other in terrible, destructive conflict. It was really urgent for the people to recover their religious faith and to learn to live together in love. You know how the story came out. Evidently, too many people paid more attention to the miracle than to the message. They didn't learn to love in time to avoid a tragedy. The old hatreds were able to take control and to divide the nation and set the people against each other. You have heard the heartbreaking stories of atrocities committed by people against their neighbors of other ethnic and religious groups. There was a terrible war. People did terrible things to those who had only recently been their neighbors. Who knows where this tragic story will end? Who knows how long the hatreds deepened by war will continue to reign?

Well, what is the point in telling that story? Simply this. We need to realize the urgency of our need to learn to love. Yes, we have all heard that Jesus commanded us to love one another. But, too often we have not taken that very seriously. We have either watered it down into something sweetly sentimental or we have thought of it as an impossible ideal. When the requirements of love conflict with our other inclinations, we usually set the requirements of love aside. Friends, we need to realize that Jesus had something very real and practical in mind when he commanded us to love and he meant it when he commanded us to do it. He commanded us to love because we need very badly to love. Our failure to love puts us in so many kinds of danger that we can't imagine them all. The commandment to love is urgent. We must not forget that.

The urgency of that need is so conspicuous that it is hard to imagine how we keep missing it. A retired Air Force general spoke to a group sharing insights he had gained in traveling widely through the world on military business. He said we no longer have a world divided between two great super powers. We have a world in which there are many little conflicts that could flare up and do destructive things to the people of the world. He specifically mentioned longstanding hatreds that exist between peoples of different ethnic and religious groups. Isn't it tragic that religious groups should be identified as the sources of hatreds? Can we believe that God wants the people of the earth to hate and destroy one another? Not if we really believe that it is Jesus who made God known.

Jesus came to tell us that God wants us to love one another. Our world has an urgent need to learn that and to follow it.

As terrible as it is, hate is still not the direct opposite of love. Indifference is. Hate at least attributes some identity to the ones who are hated. Indifference treats them as if they are not important — or as if they don't exist. That is worse. And there is lots of indifference in our world. There are lots of people who can hear that people are starving in North Korea and that thousands are dying as a result of floods and poverty in Central America and just not care. Indifference, too, can destroy. Indifference, too, is evidence of the urgency of our need to learn to love.

There is one other demonstration of our need to learn to love that is so obvious that it is scary. Our country seems always to be hovering on the brink of one military involvement or another. We could so easily be involved, at the drop of a hat, in the terrible business of killing and being killed. Most of us have grudgingly decided that it is sometimes a tragic necessity to use military force to contain aggressive destructiveness. But it is dangerous. It is seductive. It could give us the notion that military action can actually solve the world's problems. It can't. At best, it is a stop gap. It only makes matters worse before they can get better. The only real solution to the world's problems is the strategy of love. It is not easy to discover what the strategy of love will require of us in a situation like the world's present conflicts. But we must ask the question and we must be ready to follow the directions of the answer. It is God's strategy for changing the world and, ultimately, it is the only thing that will work.

The urgency of our need to learn to love is most conspicuous when we focus our attention on the massive movements of human history. But there are other evidences that are closer to us. They may be just as painful in their own ways. There are communities and schools and churches that are stagnating and becoming dysfunctional because no one cares enough to do what is needed to keep them doing what their people need for them to do. There are families that are falling apart because their members just never have really learned how to love. And there are people — lots of people — for whom life is less than real life because they have never learned to love life and to love others and to love themselves with a really healthy self-love. For people in those situations, life may muddle down into what Thoreau called "quiet desperation." They, too, have an urgent need for love. In fact, our much talked about decline in morality may be, at the bottom, a result of our inability to love ourselves with a healthy self-love and to love our neighbors.

Well, then, what is love? What is this thing that the world needs so desperately? Many of us really don't know. We talk a lot about love, but what we say about it suggests some very inadequate ideas about what it is.

Jesus has shown us what love is. He said, "This is my commandment, that you shall love each other as I have loved you." What kind of love has Jesus demonstrated? He has shown us a love that is a commitment. It is a love that wants life, real life, fullness of life, life at its best for those who are loved. And it is a love that is willing to do whatever is necessary for those who are loved to have that life no matter what it costs. That is what the cross was all about. And Jesus has shown us a love that is inclusive. It starts with a healthy self-love. Yes, it starts with wanting life at its best for yourself. It is not only permitted but necessary to love yourself. If sacrifice is necessary, it comes later, as a commitment to life, not as some kind of a sick rejection of life. But real love cannot be contained within self. Real love reaches out to embrace others and to want for them all that you want for yourself, fullness of life. Eventually real love embraces all others. It embraces the whole creation. It becomes a commitment to life for the whole creation. And that is the shape of a really active love for God. That is the kind of love Jesus has taught us. It is the kind of love with which Jesus loves us.

Can you see how that kind of loving commitment could make a difference in our lives and in our world? Can you see how enough of that kind of love might have made a difference in Bosnia? Can you see how it can make a difference in our communities and in our schools and in our churches and in our families and in our own lives? It really is the hope of the world. Love and hate have one thing in common. They both tend to multiply themselves by calling forth a similar response. Just as hate has generated responding hate and filled the country in Bosnia, so love can generate more love. If we love someone, especially someone who is lonely or angry or full of hate, that person may eventually be changed by love into someone who can love. In that way, love can fill the earth and change it. That is the strategy of Jesus for changing the world. It will work if we work it. It is the hope of the world, the only real hope.

But how can we love? With so much hate and indifference in our world — and in our lives — how can we learn to love? Who will enable us? God will. God has shown us God's love for us through Jesus. That same love reaches us through many relationships and experiences in our everyday lives. Know yourself as one who is loved by God and by others. Take that love into yourself and let it change your life. Then share it with others and become a participant in the life-shaping multiplication of love. No, it will not always be easy. It may generate painful conflicts within ourselves. It may be costly in many ways. If you have begun to imagine what love will require in some of the situations we have mentioned, you have already begun to realize that. But God will make you able. And the prize is worth the price. Love is not only the hope of the world, it is also your own only hope for fullness of life. We all have an urgent need to learn to love.

Something very significant happened recently in a little town in southeast Texas. You may have all read about the terrible thing that happened in Jasper, Texas. A small group of White men got drunk one night and did something really terrible to a Black man — just because he was Black. They dragged him to death behind a pickup truck. That is the kind of incident that can tear communities apart and set races against one another and explode into catastrophic violence. Sure enough, the representatives of hate groups from both races converged on the town to fan the flames of hostility. But the people of Jasper did not respond to them. Everyone, both Black and White, had been sickened by the terrible thing that had happened. They told the people from the hate groups to go home. They didn't have time for them. They were too busy learning to love one another and trying to rebuild their community. Many inspiring stories have come out of that tragedy demonstrating how Christian people can put their faith to work to deal with an atrocity and to be reconciled to one another. They have set the world a good example. Let us hope we will all learn to follow it before it is too late.[1]

---

1. A version of this sermon was originally published in *Pulpit Digest,* September-October, 1999, David Albert Farmer, Editor (Inver Grove Heights, Minnesota: Logos Productions Inc.).

Overcoming Evil

Romans 12:17-21

Evil is a reality. We have to cope with it. The Bible tells us what to do about evil. "Do not be overcome by evil but overcome evil with good" (Romans 12:21). That *is* the right answer. But, when we are faced with the reality of evil, it is awfully hard to do the right thing. The process that can bring us to the ability to do it is nothing less than a part of the saving work of God.

On September 11, 2001, the United States of America and the rest of the world came face to face with the reality of evil in a new and horrifying way. Millions of people watched on live television as the second of two hijacked airliners was crashed into the second tower of The World Trade Center in New York City, sending plumes of flame and smoke belching out from all sides of the building. We all knew without being told that we were witnessing a well planned and very deliberate act of terrorism. We all wondered how anyone could hate so deeply that they would be willing to do a thing like that. We were all aghast at what we saw.

After that, one emotion followed another for most of us. We knew at the time of impact that thousands of innocent people were dying. We could imagine what it would have been like to have someone in one of the planes or the towers or in the Pentagon. Our hearts hurt. We were caught up in grief. There was also admiration. The news commentators spoke of the chaos around the crash site but, miraculously, most of the mostly unprepared people who were there did exactly the right things. And a new group of heroes emerged, firemen, police officers, and others who risked their lives to snatch the lives of others out of the hands of death.

Soon we all began to experience anger, a real and righteous anger. We were angry at what happened, and at the people who made it happen and at the whole configuration of human history that contributed to its happening. And, we were right to be angry. It should not have happened.

Soon we began to realize that we have an enemy who hates us and wants to destroy us. We realized that we are up against something really evil.

A second shock wave struck us when television newscasts showed pictures of people, even little children, in what we thought were friendly countries, celebrating the catastrophe and when we heard that many in other parts of the world were saying, "It's too bad that it happened, but the Americans brought it on themselves." We are accustomed to thinking of our country as heroic and good. It is hard to discover that not everyone sees us in that way. When we heard those things, we were even more angry.

How should we respond to all of these things? There is certainly that within each of us that wants to strike back in anger, to take all of the military and economic power that our country can muster and return hurt for hurt. But there is that within many of us that really doesn't want a war. Thousands have already died. We don't want any more to die if that can be avoided. No doubt, some military response will be necessary. The enemy cannot be allowed to keep on committing atrocities. But military response alone will not solve our world's problems. One of the news commentators who reflected on the disaster quoted theologian Reinhold Niebuhr, who said, "Anger is the right response to evil. But it is important not to let anger turn into hatred or revenge." If we do, we ourselves will have been overcome by the evil we have suffered. Fear and hate and terrorism will have won.

In the months following the September 11 tragedy, the world has watched the escalation of hatred and hostilities between Israelis and Palestinians. We have seen two peoples, whose futures are tied to each other, returning hurt for hurt in a terrible spiral, until now the world wonders if they will ever be able to live in peace. We could imagine ourselves being caught up in a similar escalation of more catastrophic proportions. We know that is not what God wants to happen and we don't want it to happen either.

Then what can we do? What should be our response to the September 11 tragedy? What does our Christian heritage offer to us?

First, we should seek healing. We were right to return to our spiritual heritage and to turn to God in our anguish and pray, "O Lord, save." We need desperately to recover our wholeness. No, things can never be as they were before. In fact, the security that we once thought we had was never real. We need to find our way to a wholeness as persons and as a nation that will work in the real world. Our faith assures us that God is always at work in human history to heal and to save. We remember the promise that was given to the people of Israel in their time of brokenness. "Comfort, O comfort my people says your God. Speak tenderly to Jerusalem and cry to her that she has served her term, that her penalty is paid, that she has received from the Lord's hand double for all her sins" (Isaiah 40:1-2).

When the Soviet Union collapsed and left the United States standing alone as the most powerful nation in the world, this country entered one of the most dangerous times in its history. Everyone expects the superpower to make everything come out all right for everybody. And everyone blames the superpower when things don't come out all right for anyone. There is bound to be jealousy because some enjoy prosperity while others endure poverty and some enjoy freedom while others endure oppression. And there are real grievances because the powerful are always tempted to forget to do justice, love mercy, and walk humbly with God. Real grievances combine with jealousy to generate hatred. The danger goes with the power. It is very important to recover our religious heritage.

Once while the British Empire held the position of the world's superpower, a grand celebration was held to commemorate the diamond jubilee of Queen Victoria. It was an awesome display of the worldwide power of the British Empire. Rudyard Kipling was asked to write a poem for the occasion. He wrote "Recessional." It was a long poem that put the nation's pride into perspective and warned the people not to forget the God beneath whom they held power. The poem repeated the refrain, "Lest we forget, lest we forget."[1] We have sometimes been in danger of forgetting, haven't we?

It is important for us to renew our relationship with God who is always here to forgive our sins, to heal our hurting hearts, to enable us to reclaim our highest national commitments, and to give us the strength and the courage to go on. We will need that renewal if we are to move into today's world and act with wisdom and decisiveness.

But, does our Christian heritage not tell us that repentance must be a part of our preparation for salvation? How can we deal with the need for repentance in this situation? Must repentance come before forgiveness and healing or is it the promise of forgiveness and healing that sets us free to reckon with our need to repent? In fact, the two need to come together in the working out of God's salvation. Repentance is a gift of God's love. It is the assurance of God's promise to save that sets us free to make needed changes — and change is a part of God's saving work.

Many of us have not been able to deal with the need for repentance in the time of our anguish. We have reacted with justifiable anger when our self-righteous enemies — and our self-righteous friends — have said the September 11 tragedy was God's punishment for something we have done. The deaths of thousands of innocent people was not something God wanted to happen. We have wanted to cry out in defense of our nation.

But as the Lord makes us able, we need to ask ourselves uncomfortable questions. Have we really lived up to the commitment to liberty and justice for all that is a part of our nation's heritage, or have we just claimed liberty and justice for ourselves? Have we allowed the seduction of prosperity and pleasure to make us compromise our integrity and our commitment to human values? Have we ever, in fact, either intentionally or unintentionally, prospered at the expense of the disadvantaged peoples of the world? Have we ever been oblivious or indifferent to the oppression of others — or have we ever in any way participated in it? Have we ever been too arrogant in our exercise of our power and have we been too ready to send in the bombers, as if they could solve the problems of the world? We need to deal with those questions seriously.

It can be a good thing, even though it is often a hard thing, to see ourselves as others see us. A few months before September 11, the editor of *Zion's Herald* magazine interviewed Arund Gandhi, the grandson of Mohandas Gandhi, who is living in this country as a missionary of his grandfather's philosophy of non-violence. He said he has been watching our society being destroyed by violence. He spoke of the spread of violence as a way of life in our country. He reflected that we feel we must spend so much money on weapons of mass destruction so we can remain safe from the rest of the world, but we have accomplished exactly the opposite result. These things are only confusing us and destroying our humanity. He said, "The way we are going at the moment, I wouldn't be surprised if, in another few years, Americans will not be able to travel anywhere in the world because they are despised by everybody and because of terrorism and threats to kill them everywhere."[2] His words were frighteningly prophetic. We will be wise to ask searching questions about ourselves as a nation. Is any part of the evil we must overcome to be found within us?

But now we have to come to the question that we announced for this sermon. How can we overcome evil? We have been forced to realize that we are up against something really evil in the world and we want to know how to overcome it. It was necessary for us to wait until now to deal with that question because we need to claim God's saving grace to enable us to overcome evil — otherwise we might have been overcome by the same evil working within us and we might not have been ready to hear what Jesus and Paul have to say about how to overcome evil.

Jesus said, "Love your enemies, do good to those who hate you, bless those who curse you, pray for those who abuse you. If anyone strikes you on the cheek, offer the other also; and from anyone who takes away your coat do not withhold even your shirt. Give to everyone who begs from you; and if anyone takes away your goods, do not ask for them again. Do to others as you would have them do to you" (Luke 6:27-31).

Paul said, "Do not repay anyone evil for evil but take thought for what is noble in the sight of all. Beloved, never avenge yourselves, but leave room for the wrath of God; for it is written 'Vengeance is mine, I will repay says the Lord.' No, 'if your enemies are hungry, feed them; if they are thirsty, give them something to drink; for by doing this, you will heap burning coals on their heads.' Do not be overcome by evil, but overcome evil with good" (Romans 12:17-21).

That is not exactly the first solution we would have thought of, is it? Yes, it is sometimes necessary to contain violence with violence. Military action against terrorism is probably necessary. But it will never solve the problem. And the longer we depend upon military action for our solution, the harder the problem will be to solve.

The real evil, the real enemy that we are up against, is hate. Hate is what makes a person fly an airplane full of people into a building full of people in an attempt to destroy as much as he can. Osama bin Laden is a real problem. But he is not the real enemy. The real enemy is the hate that burns within him and others like him. In a sense, he, too, is the victim of hate. Yes, he is responsible for what he did under the compulsion of hate, just as we will be responsible for anything we do under the compulsion of hate if we allow hate to grow within us. But, if we allow hate to grow within us, we will have been overcome by evil and hate will have won.

The only way to overcome hate is with love. At first, that sounds like an irresponsible platitude. If it is ever to be more than that, we are going to have to learn a lot more about the dynamics of love and about how to put love to work in our world than we know now — but it is long past time for us to start learning. It is clear that we will have to be made able to love through some miraculous saving work of God. But that miracle can and does happen. Love will require us to learn respect and understanding in situations in which those attitudes are very hard to maintain. And love will require us to take action to change those conditions that generate hate. A part of our nation's first announced strategy in dealing with terrorism had to do with the rehabilitation of a nation so impoverished and devastated by its succession of wars that it was reduced to desperation that gave birth to hate. We need to remember that an effective strategy for overcoming hate may indeed involve feeding our enemies.

What else must we learn about love? What else will love teach us about how to overcome evil? We will learn as we go. But it really is the only way to go. Love really is the only hope for our world. Friends, let us not be overcome by evil. Let us learn how to overcome evil with good.

---

1. Rudyard Kipling, "Recessional" from *The Five Nations* (Doubleday, Doran & Company Inc., 1903) or see *The Methodist Hymnal*, 1932, p. 497.

2. Arund Gandhi, from an interview published in *Zion's Herald*, July-August, 2001, (New Berwick, Minnesota: Boston Wesleyan Association), pp. 16-18, 30-31.

The Shaking Of The Foundations

Jeremiah 4:23-26

It is a good thing to stop from time to time in the presence of God and to look back and to look around and to reflect on what has been happening to us and to our world and to ask what it means. When I look back in that way over the past two or three years, I find myself remembering the title of a sermon preached by theologian Paul Tillich back in the 1940s. The sermon was on "The Shaking of the Foundations."[1]

Tillich was reflecting upon some passages from the writings of the prophets Isaiah and Jeremiah. The people of Israel were living through a time when the foundations of everything they had relied upon seemed to be shaking. Everything seemed to be falling apart. The people had felt proud in their belief that they were the chosen people of God and secure in their prosperity. But the spiritual infrastructure of their nation had withered away and their country was in the process of falling under the oppression of foreign enemies. The prophets spoke words from the Lord that were appropriate for their people in that day.

Tillich believed that his own world was going through a time of the shaking of foundations. He had seen the optimism with which the twentieth century began devastated by the experiences of two world wars and the threat of nuclear holocaust. He believed that the message of the prophets was appropriate for people in his own day.

I think that many of us are experiencing our present situation in life as a time when the foundations of all that we have put our trust in are shaking. Many of the things we thought we could depend upon seem to be in danger of falling apart. It just may be that the word from the Lord that the prophets delivered in their day will have a message for us, too.

Have you been feeling the foundations shaking? Lots of us have. We can remember a time not long ago when the Soviet Union disintegrated, leaving our country as the world's only superpower. Instead of humbly learning the lesson that superpowers can disintegrate, we were proud, as if we had won a contest. We have always thought of ourselves as the heroic advocates of some high human values learned from our Judeo-Christian religious heritage. We rather thought those values had won us a victory. We settled down into feeling secure. We thought we had nothing better to do than to prosper.

Then September 11, 2001, came. We all saw the twin towers of The World Trade Center in New York come crashing down, crushing out the lives of thousands of innocent people. Suddenly we realized that we are not secure. Suddenly we realized that there are millions of people in our world who hate us and millions more who do not hold the same noble and heroic image of our country that we hold. The foundations began to shake.

Before we had gotten over the shock of the terrorist attack, we got news of the collapse of the Enron corporation as a result of the exploitative mismanagement of their top executives. Other similar failures followed. These failures exposed the fact that certain practices that undermined the integrity of the stock market had become accepted — some thought even necessary — in American business. It became apparent that those practices had at least some tacit support from the regulatory agencies and even of the government of the United States. Thousands were robbed of their life savings and, in the aftermath, virtually every person and institution in our country lost a major piece of its prosperity. In one way, this was even more devastating than 9-11. The terrorist attack was an act of a foreign enemy. The fall of Enron and the revelations that followed it were acts of treachery by people and structures of business and government that we had trusted and that we need to be able to trust. The foundations are shaking.

And now we are in a war. At their best, wars are all morally ambiguous and destructive things. If we ever go to war without feeling both the pain of our own people and the pain of our enemies, we will have lost a part of our humanity. The ambiguities surrounding this war have provoked worldwide protests, alienated us from some of our best friends, and cast a shadow over our country's ability to give moral leadership in the world. The foundations are shaking.

If we pay attention, we can see the foundations of many other important structures of life shaking. Statistics on divorce and teen pregnancies show us that the foundations of family life are shaking. The previews of coming attractions in any movie theater will show us that the structures of morality in our society are shaking. And there are conspicuous evidences that many of the other structures of community and business life that we need to depend upon are being damaged by neglect or by exploitation. The foundations are shaking. You have been feeling it, haven't you?

Can we imagine what things were like for the people of Israel as they felt the foundations of their way of life trembling? Could the words from the Lord spoken by the prophets Jeremiah and Isaiah have something important to say to us? Let's listen to see.

First, Jeremiah called the people to look honestly at what was happening to them and to learn what it would teach them. The shaking of the foundations teaches us that all of the structures of human life are vulnerable and we are all mortal. Only God is immortal. Tillich said that it was only the prophets who could dare to reckon honestly with what was happening to their beloved nation. They could do it only because they were in touch with the one who really is invulnerable, the eternal God.

Many were unwilling — or unable — to hear the message the prophets brought. Some because they just couldn't deal with their own mortality, some because they wanted just to keep on doing business as usual. They called the prophets unpatriotic. But the prophets condemned those who tried to gloss over the reality. Jeremiah said, "They have treated the wounds of my people carelessly, saying, 'Peace, peace,' where there is no peace" (Jeremiah 6:14).

There are no structures of human life, no economic power, no military might, no religious tradition that is beyond the vulnerability that comes with human mortality — not in Israel — not in America — not anywhere. Those who are wise will see the shaking of the foundations and know what it means. They will build their lives on a relationship with that one who alone is not vulnerable, the eternal God. Those who do that will be free, as the prophets were free, to look honestly at what is happening to us and to act appropriately.

The prophet's message always includes a call to repentance. We always resist that. We are always quick to insist upon our own rightness. But we should always at least ask if there is anything of which we need to repent. I do not believe for a minute that God sent the terrorists to attack The World Trade Center to bring our nation to its knees. That was something that God did not want to happen. But God often uses things that should not have happened to show us things that we need to see. We always ought to ask, "Is there anything of which we need to repent?"

The prophets charged the people of Israel with forsaking their covenant with God. No, they hadn't closed the Temple. They were still paying lip service to their religious tradition. But they weren't letting it shape their lives. Jeremiah represented the Lord saying, "My people have committed two evils. They have forsaken me, the fountain of living water and have dug our cisterns for themselves, broken cisterns that can hold no water" (Jeremiah 2:13). Right now, there are many of us who would fight for the right to keep on pledging allegiance to "One nation, under God, indivisible, with liberty and justice for all." But is that a real commitment for us or just a hallowed tradition? There is another creed that is seldom recited but often taught that says, "Material wealth is the really important thing. Do whatever you have to do to get it and don't worry about the impact on anyone else." You have seen that creed in practice, haven't you? Could its practice have contributed to the conditions that have set the foundations to shaking? Which of the affirmations are we really allowing to shape our lives and the life of our nation? Is there anything of which we need to repent? We should always ask.

But the prophet's message is always ultimately a message of promise. Both the Old Testament and the New are based on the belief that God is alive and at work in our world, at work in love, at work to save. And this salvation is not just a matter of saving people out of the world and into heaven. It is also a matter of God saving people and peoples from the destruction they keep bringing upon themselves and moving them toward the fulfillment of God's higher purpose for us all. The God who was made known through Jesus Christ has been at work to save since the beginning of time. Jeremiah said, "I know the plans I have for you, says the Lord, plans for your welfare and not for harm, to give you a future of hope" (Jeremiah 29:11).

Can you see God at work in our world to save? Can you see God's hand at work in something like the fall of the Berlin Wall and in the ending of apartheid in South Africa? Can you believe that God was at work as Czechoslovakia accomplished the peaceful partitioning of their country without any of the violence that devastated Yugoslavia? Can you see God at work to save through groups of high school students working to prevent teen suicides, or in groups of church people caring for people with AIDS?

The saving work of God is not always conspicuous or quick. Real salvation usually can't be. But we need to learn to believe that is going on — and to wait upon it — and to recognize it when it happens.

It is important for us to be able to recognize the saving work of God when it happens because God calls us to participate in it. Jeremiah spent much of his prophecy trying to teach the people of Israel how to live through the tumultuous things that were happening in their history so that they could participate in the saving work that God was trying to do (Jeremiah 29:1-14). The instructions could not be simple. The call to participate in God's saving work was addressed to us more clearly by Jesus who said, "If any want to become my followers, let them deny themselves and take up their cross and follow me" (Matthew 16:24).

Part of participating in God's saving work may be a matter of trusting God to save and waiting upon God's action rather than rushing to try to solve all of the world's problems by the same old solutions that have been making matters worse through the centuries, using more manipulation to help the stock market recover, or trying to solve the problem of hate with military action. The Lord may have some better ways to save. We have to wait upon them and be open to them.

The most important thing to remember is that God is a God of love and God works in love to save. God calls us to learn to love and to participate in God's loving work. As we learn to live in love, we will recover some things that we seem to have lost, things like integrity and responsibility, and we just may discover some entirely new ways of solving the problems of this world whose foundations keep shaking.

Paul Tillich ended his sermon on the shaking of the foundations with a reference to a passage from the prophecy of Isaiah. "Lift up your eyes to the heavens, and look at the earth beneath; for the heavens will vanish like smoke, the earth will wear out like a garment, and those who live on it will die like gnats; but my salvation will be forever, and my deliverance will never be ended" (Isaiah 51:6). In times when the foundations of everything we have relied upon seem to be shaking and things seem to be falling apart, would we not be wise to get in touch with the one who alone is eternal and find ways of becoming participants in the saving work of God? Could it be that this is what the Lord requires of us?

---

1. Paul Tillich, *The Shaking Of The Foundations* (New York: Charles Scribner's Sons, 1948), pp.1-11.

Appendix:
Questions For Group Discussion

Once To Every Man And Nation
Topic: Call To Involvement

1. How do you feel about the idea that Christians are called to take decisive action and to make a difference in the world?
2. What big issues do you see facing the nation or the world that call for some Christian action?
3. What sorts of things can Christian people and churches do to make a difference in the world? Are there any kinds of action that you think Christians ought not to take?
4. Whom have you known or known of who took some kind of costly or dangerous action in the service of truth and justice?

God's "No"
Topic: Judgment Of God

1. List the things upon which you think God's "No" must be resting.
2. When have you had to do something upon which you felt God's "No" resting? (You may want to accomplish this sharing anonymously by having each person write his or her answer on a sheet of paper or card, then collecting, shuffling, and redistributing the cards so that each person reads the answer of another person.)
3. Discuss what Christians should do in situations like the ones just shared.
4. How did you feel about what this meditation said about war? (Save this question until last. Don't let it dominate the whole discussion.)

How Can I Love My Country?
Topic: Christian Patriotism

1. In what ways do you feel called to help your country become what God wants it to be?
2. In what ways do you feel called to cry out against some wrongness in your country?
3. In what ways do you feel required to stand with your country under the judgment of God and to share the suffering that results from its wrongness?

Christian Citizenship In A Pluralistic Society
Topic: Pluralism

1. If you were a Christian family living in a Muslim country, what kinds of respect would you want that country and your Muslim neighbors to show for your religion? What would it mean for us to show similar respect for people who practice other religions while living in our country?
2. What would it mean for us to resist the establishment of secularism as our country's state religion without asking for the establishment of our own religion?
3. Whom do you know who practices the Christian faith in an influential way while respecting the religion of others?

Economic Justice, Facing The Issue
Topic: Economic Justice

1. Can you see that the world's economic processes are working in a way that makes the rich richer and the poor poorer?
2. Have you traveled and seen the impact of this on people in developing countries? Tell about it.
3. List the things you have seen in your own country that are evidences of this process.
4. Have you seen that the Bible requires economic justice?
5. What would economic justice in our world look like?
6. What can lay Christians do to work toward economic justice?

Adam And Evie

Topic: Materialism

1. Can you identify with Adam and Evie?
2. What do you think about the two different attitudes toward ambition expressed in the meditation?
3. If you participated in the discussion on economic justice, can you see the relationship between the two meditations?
4. How can we use our good fortune to make life better for others as well as for ourselves?

Creative Management Of The Earth

Topic: Ecology

1. How seriously do you take the reports of the threats to our environment?
2. Which environmental concerns seem most urgent to you?
3. Could we ever really adopt the idea of stewardship with responsibility to manage instead of ownership with the right to exploit as our understanding of our relationship with the earth?
4. Can you see that our addiction to affluence is a source of many of our world's problems? Do you think we can ever be saved from it?
5. Should we really be free to do anything we want to?

On Sharing Leadership

Topic: Gender Roles

1. List those aspects of the changes in gender roles you have seen that you think are good.
2. List the aspects of the changes you have seen in gender roles that you think may not be good.
3. Are you having trouble adjusting to some of the changes that you know are good?
4. The meditation describes a way of living and working that allows every person to become the unique person he or she can be and to make his or her best contribution and that calls everyone to live and work together appreciating and respecting the

unique contribution of others. Talk for a while about the shape that might take in the family, in business, and in the church.

5. Where have you seen destructive effects coming from people's confinement within traditional gender roles?

Weep For The Children
Topic: Child Advocacy

1. Share your memories of situations in which you saw children suffering neglect or abuse because of the sinfulness of the world.
2. List the ways you know of in which people can become redemptively involved in the lives of "at risk" children.
3. List the major social and political issues before your community and nation that would have a bearing on the well-being of children.
4. What can we do to reach out in love to children who suffer in other parts of the world?

What Will You Do With Your Freedom?
Topic: Abstinence

1. Allow three minutes of silence for each member of the group to count the people whom he or she knows who have had any kind of a serious problem with gambling or tobacco or alcohol or other drugs. Then share the number, (not the names), and add up the total.
2. Can you see that the acceptability of these things causes some people to be tripped into self-destructive behavior?
3. How big a change in your life would be required for you to become an abstainer from gambling and the use of alcohol and other drugs?
4. Could you become an abstainer and an advocate of abstinence without taking an offensive, superior attitude toward others who don't?

Feeding God's Sheep

Topic: Youth In Today's Society

1. Make a list of all of the young people who are parts of your life or who are within reach of your life.
2. Identify those who seem to be having a hard time with some aspect of their growing up.
3. Identify those on both lists who might be open to some adult friendship from you.
4. Make a plan for how you can be lovingly involved in the lives of these youth.
5. After allowing ten minutes for each group member to go through this process, share with the group the plans you have made without sharing the identity of the young people you have in mind.

Thinking About Suicide

Topic: Suicide

1. Ask how many members of the group have ever been really close to someone who committed suicide. Answer with a show of hands.
2. Make a list of the answers you found in the meditation to questions you have had about suicide. Share both the questions and the answers with the group.
3. Share the questions you have about suicide for which you still have not found answers. Discuss them with the group.

The Radicalizing Of Charlie

Topics: Abortion, Decisiveness

1. With which of the characters in the drama did you find yourself identifying?
2. Go around the circle and let each person summarize his or her beliefs about abortion. If this is uncomfortable, let each person write out a brief statement on a card. Collect the cards, shuffle them, redistribute them, and read them anonymously.
3. What should the church be doing about the abortion issue?
4. Are those who are unwilling to be radicalized always destined to be indecisive?

A Question Of Right And Wrong
Topic: Moral Relativism

1. Are you aware of the increasingly relativistic moral climate in which we live? How do you feel about it?
2. How do you feel when someone else tells you what you ought to do or not to do?
3. Is there really one who is beyond us all whom we ought to obey? Does God really know best?
4. How can we know that we know the will of God?
5. How can we communicate high expectations of others, especially leaders, without trying to impose our beliefs upon them?

Homosexuality, Facing The Issue
Topic: Homosexuality

1. By a show of hands, ask how many members of the group are personally acquainted with someone whom they either know to be or suspect of being homosexual. Beyond this, do not identify the people.
2. By a show of hands, ask how many have any ambivalence about whether or not the homosexual lifestyle can ever be made compatible with the Christian faith. Invite any who wish to do so to explain their feelings.
3. What does it mean to treat homosexual people as persons of sacred worth even if you do not feel that you can condone their lifestyle?
4. Can you see how the church is caught in a conflict between morality and compassion on this issue? Discuss how this conflict can be resolved.
5. If you know a homosexual person who is willing to do so, ask him or her to come and discuss the issue with you.

Return From A Far Country

Topic: Moral Choice

1. Could you identify at all with the young man in the story?
2. Are you conscious of the change in lifestyles and values that have taken place in our country in recent years?
3. Can you see the relationship between love and the lifestyle of hard work, moral discipline, and religious tradition?
4. What kinds of changes are really needed and how can they best be made?

A Leper In Our Path

Topic: AIDS

1. What is your natural response to HIV/AIDS and to people who have it? How do they make you feel?
2. Can you bring yourself to make a compassionate response to someone who is suffering, even if they are suffering as a result of doing something you think is wrong?
3. Are you aware of any agency in your community through which volunteers can become involved in a compassionate ministry to people who have AIDS?
4. Besides participating in personal ministries of compassion, what could your church do to work against the spread of AIDS and to provide needed care for the victims? What can the church do about the worldwide AIDS epidemic?

War Against Hate

Topic: Hate

1. How do you feel about the idea that hate is the great enemy of humankind?
2. How do you feel about the description of the dynamics of love, indifference, and hate that are included in the meditation? Have you seen things working that way or have you not?
3. How can we seek to be saved from hatred in our own lives?
4. How can we work to overcome hatred in others?

Breaking Down Walls
Topic: Race Relations

1. Are you aware that dividing walls of hostility still exist between races? How important is that to you?
2. List as many of the sources of hurt and hostility as you can. Try hard to see the sources of hurt on both sides of the color line. If yours is an interracial group, this would be a good time and place to start talking and listening. If it is not, maybe you will want to invite some members of another race to participate in this discussion.
3. After you have built your lists, deal with the question, "How does this make you feel?"
4. Finally, spend a few minutes brainstorming about how you can make things better.

Landsberg
Topic: War

1. Did the story of the chapel service in Landsberg trigger any memories or reflections in you? Share them.
2. Have you ever given any serious thought to what it would mean to take love and reconciliation seriously as a strategy for solving the world's problems? Talk about that.
3. Pick one of the situations of violent conflict in the world today and think together about how reconciliation might be accomplished in it.

Message From Medjugorje
Topic: The Urgency Of Love

1. Do you believe that love really can be a practical solution to the world's problems?
2. In what real life situations in the world today do you see the most urgent need for love?
3. In what painful situations of conflict have you seen love make a difference for good?

Overcoming Evil
Topic: 9/11

1. Start by going around the room and letting each person share, first, what they thought when they first learned of the 9/11 attack, and then, what they are thinking and feeling about it now.
2. By a show of hands, count how many feel that they are coming to terms with their anger.
3. By a show of hands, count how many think our country can grow in faith and in wisdom through this experience.
4. By a show of hands, count how many now feel free to talk about things of which our country may need to repent.
5. In discussion, talk about the ways in which we might be able to overcome evil with good.

The Shaking Of The Foundations
Topic: Morally Responsible Life In A Changing World

1. How many of the group members feel that they are experiencing the shaking of the foundations of their way of life? Respond by a show of hands. Then discuss the experiences that have caused them to feel that.
2. In what ways do you think the nation should "return to the fountain of living water"?
3. Can the group members visualize God working to save through the events in our lives and through the movements of human history? Is this a new understanding of the saving work of God for the group? Can you see that it is biblical?
4. In which of the things that are going on in our world do you see God working to save?
5. In what ways might we become participants in what God is doing in the world?